INSIGHT FOR LIVING BIB
INSIGHTS AND APPLICATIO

REVELATION
UNVEILING THE END

ACT **3**

The FINAL *Curtain*

FROM THE BIBLE-TEACHING MINISTRY OF
CHARLES R. SWINDOLL

INSIGHT FOR LIVING

REVELATION—UNVEILING THE END, ACT 3
The Final Curtain

Bible Companion

FROM THE BIBLE-TEACHING MINISTRY OF CHARLES R. SWINDOLL

Charles R. Swindoll has devoted his life to the clear, practical teaching and application of God's Word and His grace. A pastor at heart, Chuck has served as senior pastor to congregations in Texas, Massachusetts, and California. He currently pastors Stonebriar Community Church in Frisco, Texas, but Chuck's listening audience extends far beyond a local church body. As a leading program in Christian broadcasting, *Insight for Living* airs in major Christian radio markets around the world, reaching people groups in languages they can understand. Chuck's extensive writing ministry has also served the body of Christ worldwide and his leadership as president and now chancellor of Dallas Theological Seminary has helped prepare and equip a new generation for ministry. Chuck and Cynthia, his partner in life and ministry, have four grown children and ten grandchildren.

Based on the original outlines, charts, and transcripts of Charles R. Swindoll's sermons, the Bible Companion text was developed and written by Mark Gaither, Th.M., Dallas Theological Seminary, and Michael J. Svigel, Th.M., Ph.D. candidate, Dallas Theological Seminary.

Editor in Chief: Cynthia Swindoll, President, Insight for Living
Executive Vice President: Wayne Stiles, Th.M., D.Min., Dallas Theological Seminary
Director of Creative Ministries: Michael J. Svigel, Th.M., Ph.D. candidate, Dallas Theological Seminary
Editors: Brie Engeler, B.A., University Scholars, Baylor University
　　　Amy Snedaker, B.A., English, Rhodes College
Copy Editors: Jim Craft, M.A., English, Mississippi College
　　　Melanie Munnell, M.A., Humanities, The University of Texas at Dallas
Proofreader: Joni Halpin, B.S., Accountancy, Miami University
Project Coordinator, Creative Ministries: Cari Harris, B.A., Journalism, Grand Canyon University
Project Coordinator, Communications: Dusty R. Crosby, B.S., Communication, Dallas Baptist University
Cover Designer: Steven Tomlin, Embry-Riddle Aeronautical University, 1992–1995
Production Artists: Sharon D. Chandler, B.A., German, Texas Tech University
　　　Nancy Gustine, B.F.A., Advertising Art, University of North Texas
Cover Images: Sky photo—Comstock, Inc.
　　　Olive branch—Alex Slobodkin
　　　Jerusalem photo—Todd Bolen/BiblePlaces.com

Published by IFL Publishing House, A Division of Insight for Living
Post Office Box 251007, Plano, Texas 75025-1007

ISBN: 978-1-57972-738-3
Printed in the United States of America

TABLE OF CONTENTS

A Letter from Chuck

When the curtain closed on the second act of our end-times trilogy, the situation looked bleak. The evil Antichrist and fiendish false prophet had taken center stage, trampling underfoot the sacred city and suffering saints (Revelation 11–13), attempting to derail God's plan and destroy His people. To the uninformed, it would appear that evil might win a shocking victory after all.

Yet as the house lights dim and the curtain parts for the final act of this apocalyptic drama, the tide decisively turns. At center stage, standing on Mount Zion, we see not a gruesome Beast conquering the saints, but the glorious Lamb standing with His elect. And in the next several chapters we'll witness God's wrath unleashed on wickedness, the defeat of the ultimate evil empire, and the establishment of a perfect kingdom of righteousness and peace.

Amidst the prophetic visions of Babylon, Armageddon, and the earthly reign of Christ, we will also see profound and practical truths that affect us today. As history rushes toward its final destiny, all of us are called to live in light of our final destination.

Brace yourself for God's last words on the last days—but don't be dismayed by the startling images of judgment and wrath. Thankfully, when the final curtain drops on human history, all creation will bow before Christ the King in a glorious new heaven and new earth.

Charles R. Swindoll

How to Use This Bible Companion

As we open the final act of God's end-times drama, we find ourselves in the midst of an intimidating torrent of visions and symbols. Indeed, no other book of the Bible has evoked greater fascination and controversy than Revelation—and the final chapters contain some of the most vivid images in Scripture. Yet when we understand the puzzling passages of this book, our lives will be impacted by practical truth. This Bible Companion is designed to help you understand John's visions of the future in the context of your life today. Many people forget that the truth communicated in the book of Revelation is not only something to be studied, but something to be *lived*.

A brief introduction to the overall structure of each lesson will help you get the most out of these studies, whether you choose to complete this study individually or as part of a group.

Lesson Organization

Each of the fifteen lessons begins with **THE HEART OF THE MATTER**, which highlights the main idea of the lesson for rapid orientation. The lesson itself is then composed of three main teaching sections: "You Are Here," "Discovering the Way," and "Starting Your Journey."

YOU ARE HERE includes an introduction and thought-provoking questions to orient you to the topic that will be examined in the lesson.

DISCOVERING THE WAY explores the principles of Scripture through observation and interpretation of the Bible passages and drawing out practical principles for life. Parallel passages and additional questions supplement the main Scriptures for more in-depth study.

STARTING YOUR JOURNEY focuses on application to help you put into practice the principles of the lesson in ways that fit your personality, gifts, and level of spiritual maturity.

USING THE BIBLE COMPANION

Revelation—Unveiling the End, Act 3 Bible Companion is designed with both individual study and small-group use in mind. Here's the method we recommend:

Prayer—Begin each lesson with prayer, asking God to teach you through His Word and open your heart to the self-discovery afforded by the questions and text of the lesson.

Scripture—Have your Bible handy. We recommend the *New American Standard Bible* or another literal translation, rather than a paraphrase. As you progress through each lesson, you'll be prompted to read relevant sections of Scripture and answer questions related to the topic. You will also want to look up Scripture passages noted in parentheses.

Questions—As you encounter the questions, approach them wisely and creatively. Not every question will be applicable to each person all the time. If you can't answer a question, continue on in the lesson. Use the questions as general guides in your thinking rather than rigid forms to complete. If there are things you just don't understand or that you want to explore further, be sure to jot down your thoughts or questions.

Features—Throughout the chapters, you'll find several special features designed to add insight or depth to your study. Use these features to enhance your study and deepen your knowledge of Scripture, history, and theology. An explanation of each feature can be found beginning on page xi.

A SPECIAL NOTE FOR SMALL GROUPS

If you have chosen to complete this study in a small-group format, carefully consider the following suggestions:

Preparation—All group members should try to prepare in advance by working through the lessons as described in the previous section. If you serve as the leader, you should take additional steps to supplement your preparation either by listening to the corresponding sermons (available for purchase at www.insight.org) or by reading any of the recommended resources. Mastery of the material will build your confidence and competence, and approaching the topic from various perspectives will equip you to freely guide discussion.

Discussion Questions—You should feel free to mold the lesson according to the needs of your unique group. At a minimum, however, the group should cover the questions marked by the group icons in each of the three main sections during your meeting time. While planning the lesson, you will want to mark additional questions you feel fit the time allotment, needs, and interests of your group. The questions are divided to assist you in your lesson preparation. Note that series of questions marked by the clock icon are *primary*— meant to contribute to a solid understanding of the lesson. The unmarked series of questions are *secondary*—intended to provide a deeper exploration of the topic and corresponding Scripture passages. Encourage your group members to dig into these questions on their own.

Flexibility—During group time, open in prayer, then lead the group through the lesson you planned in advance. Members may want to share their own answers to the questions, contribute their insights, or steer the discussion in a particular direction that fits the needs of the group. Sometimes group members will want to discuss questions you may have left out of the planned lesson. *Be flexible*, but try to stay on schedule so the group has sufficient time for the final section, "Starting Your Journey," where the application of the lesson begins.

Goal—If it's unrealistic for your group to complete a single lesson during a session, consider continuing where you left off in the next session. The goal is not merely to cover material but to promote in-depth, personal discussion of the topic with a view toward personal response and application. To do this, the group will need to both understand the biblical principles and apply them to their lives.

Our prayer is that the biblical principles, exercises, and applications in this Bible Companion will help you not only to understand the meaning of the book of Revelation but also to apply the truth it contains to your life.

SPECIAL BIBLE COMPANION FEATURES

Lessons are supplemented with a variety of special features to summarize and clarify teaching points or to provide opportunities for more advanced study. Although they are not essential for understanding and applying the principles in the lesson, they will offer valuable nuggets of insight as you work through this material.

GETTING TO THE ROOT
While our English versions of the Scriptures are reliable, studying the original languages can often bring to light nuances of the text that are sometimes missed in translation. This feature explores the meaning of the underlying Hebrew or Greek words or phrases in a particular passage, sometimes providing parallel examples to illuminate the meaning of the inspired text.

DIGGING DEEPER
Various passages in Scripture touch on deeper theological questions or confront modern worldviews and philosophies that conflict with a biblical world-view. This feature will help you gain deeper insight into specific theological issues related to the biblical text.

DOORWAY TO HISTORY
Sometimes the chronological gap that separates us from the original author and readers clouds our understanding of a passage of Scripture. This feature takes you back in time to explore the surrounding history, culture, and customs of the world in which Revelation was written.

REVELATION
UNVEILING THE END

ACT 3

The FINAL *Curtain*

A SURPRISING PREVIEW OF COMING ATTRACTIONS

Revelation 14:1–13

THE HEART OF THE MATTER

Revelation 14 provides a preview of specific end-times events, delivering encouragement to believers and a hard warning to unbelievers. God neither forgets His own nor allows the wicked to escape without facing severe consequences. We can rejoice over those triumphant saints who will receive great rewards and also find relief in the reassurance that God is master even over those who work against Him.

In preparation for this lesson, read Revelation 14:1–13.

YOU ARE HERE

"Coming soon . . ."

Those words excite our senses, enliven our curiosity, and arouse a sense of wonder. The entertainment industry capitalizes on people's desire to get a sneak peek at coming attractions. Magazines run sections that whet the reader's appetite for the next issue. Television ads can rouse an audience with just a few rapid-fire scenes from an upcoming episode. And "teaser trailers" find their way into theaters sometimes months before filmmakers have finished making the movie.

However, we all know the disappointment that can come when the reality fails to live up to the hype. Thankfully, the preview of future events given by God in the book of Revelation will never disappoint. The Lord *never* cuts corners on His promises.

Why do you think people want to know what the future holds? List several specific reasons.

_____

_____

_____

If you were given the opportunity to see your future, would you take it? Why, or why not? How many details about the future would you want to know?

_____

_____

_____

How does it make you feel to know that only God knows the future completely?

_____

_____

_____

In His infinite wisdom, God has given us a preview of coming attractions. He alone knows the future. However, because He also *controls* the future, these glimpses are not meant to simply enliven our curiosity. They're given to warn those who choose to reject Christ and to encourage believers in Christ to live a life of faith until He returns. Knowing the God who holds the future in His hands should impact how we live today. Though we cannot change the course of the future, we can let the truth about the future change us.

 **DISCOVERING THE WAY**

In the historical sections of Scripture such as Genesis or the Gospels, the story generally unfolds in chronological order. However, in prophetic Scriptures the reader is often taken on a literary journey that moves in and out of chronological order. The order of the visions in Revelation does not always follow the actual sequence of events that will play out in the future. Sometimes a vision will describe the Tribulation as a whole. Other times it will portray a series of judgments fulfilled in order. Occasionally the vision will back up and fill in detailed information or jump forward to preview what will come. A brief review of end-times chronology and its relationship to the visions in the book of Revelation will help us get oriented.

CLARIFICATION OF PROPHETIC CHRONOLOGY

If you have studied the book of Revelation previously, try to outline or chart the major sections and visions in the book. If you have never studied the book before, leave this and the next question blank.

Now try to draw a timeline of end-times events, including at least the following: the rapture, the seven-year Tribulation, the coming of the two witnesses, the rise of the Beast and False Prophet, the return of Christ, the thousand-year reign, the final judgment, and the eternal state.

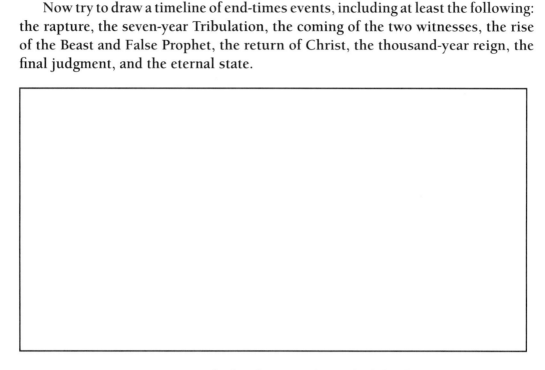

Compare your answers with the charts at the end of this lesson, making any corrections necessary.

The book of Revelation can be divided into three major chronological divisions according to Christ's own words in Revelation 1:19—the things which John saw (1:9–20), the things which are (2:1–3:22), and the things which will take place in the future (4:1–22:5). Within the large section that covers events yet future, we read of John's astonishing vision of the heavenly throne room with a focus on Christ as judge (4:1–5:14), who opens a seven-sealed scroll that reveals the first judgments of the coming Tribulation period (6:1–8:1). Within this series of judgments, a brief interlude highlights a protected Jewish remnant as well as a great multitude of Gentiles who will be converted to Christ during the Tribulation (7:1–17). The seventh seal initiates the seven trumpet judgments (8:2–11:19). A brief interlude comes in the midst of these judgments and focuses on the prophetic mission of God's two witnesses (11:1–14). The vision of Revelation 12–13 introduces seven major characters who will play important roles in the drama of the Tribulation: the Dragon (Satan), the Woman (Israel), the Male Child (Christ), the Archangel (Michael), the rest of the Woman's offspring (Tribulation believers), the Beast from the sea (the Antichrist), and the Beast from the earth (the false prophet).

As the curtain closed on Act 2 of this great end-times drama, the world was suffering at the brutal hands of the Antichrist. An epidemic of deception, destruction, and devastation poisoned humanity, and the ominous clouds of the most severe judgments gathered on the horizon. (For more information, read *Revelation—Unveiling the End, Act 2: The Earthly Drama Bible Companion* [Plano, Tex.: IFL Publishing House, 2006].)

After a brief pause, the final curtain opens on Act 3 of God's story of cosmic redemption. And, fittingly, the Lamb of God again takes center stage.

PORTRAIT OF TRIUMPHANT SAINTS (REVELATION 14:1–5)

The fourteenth chapter of Revelation provides an overture for the end. In this thematic preview of coming attractions, we step closer to the end of the Great Tribulation and learn how God will judge the wicked and honor His saints.

The 144,000 people in the preserved remnant of Israel will someday stand with Jesus Christ on Mount Zion—in the earthly city of Jerusalem (Revelation 14:1; compare with 7:1–8). Though they will be attacked by the Antichrist during the Great Tribulation (11:1–2), ethnic Israel will be preserved during this time (12:14), to be gathered together once more when the Lord returns to earth to establish His kingdom.

In John's vision, while he observed this glorious gathering of saints on Mount Zion, music began to pour forth from heaven (Revelation 14:2–3). Only the 144,000 will understand the celestial chorus, for they are the firstfruits of the Messianic kingdom—God's select and chosen few who will see the fulfillment of His ancient promise that Israel would be a blessing to all nations (Genesis 26:4).

The themes of Revelation 14 mirror certain ideas in Old Testament prophecies. Read the following passages, and note what they say about Mount Zion, or Jerusalem, and Israel.

Psalm 2:1–6

_____

_____

_____

Isaiah 24:21–23

_____

_____

_____

Isaiah 37:31–32

_____

_____

_____

Joel 3:16–17

_____

_____

_____

Micah 4:6–8

_____

_____

_____

Based on these Old Testament passages, what do you think the symbol of the 144,000 standing on Mount Zion with the Lamb represents in God's fulfillment of end-times prophecy?

_____

_____

_____

SERIES OF HEAVENLY ANNOUNCEMENTS (REVELATION 14:6–13)

After Revelation gives us a glimpse of the remnant of Israel standing with Christ on Mount Zion, the stage clears and the backdrop changes as we read of another series of climactic announcements.

The announcements John heard do not appear in chronological order; they deal with themes and events that stretch across the Tribulation period and find their ultimate climax at the end of time. The first angel announces the eternal "good news," calling all people to worship God the Creator rather than Satan, who will soon be judged (Revelation 14:6–7).

The second angel announces in advance that "Babylon the great" has fallen (Revelation 14:8). A detailed description of that future judgment awaits us in Revelation 15–18. With the fall of the evil religious, political, and economic system called "Babylon," all those who follow in its path will also fall.

The third angel pronounces judgment on all those who fail to believe the eternal gospel and come into a right relationship with Jesus Christ by faith. They will suffer eternal torment (Revelation 14:9–11). The stakes could not be higher nor the consequences more severe. Willfully worshiping the Beast and taking his mark will seal one's fate.

DIGGING DEEPER
Is Eternal Punishment Biblical?

The concept of never-ending, conscious punishment for unbelievers is unpopular among some Christians. They would prefer to believe that all people are forgiven and will go to heaven one day (universalism) or that the unsaved will simply be destroyed rather than continue existing forever (annihilationism). Others see the lake of fire as figurative or metaphorical rather than literal.[1]

Admittedly, the doctrine of never-ending, conscious punishment of the lost is a difficult one to accept mentally and emotionally. However, the Bible is clear that those who choose not to have their sins forgiven through faith in Christ will suffer for eternity in the place prepared for the Devil and his angels (Matthew 25:41). Also, we are told the clear fate of those who will worship the Beast during the Tribulation: "And the smoke of their torment goes up forever and ever; they have no rest day and night" (Revelation 14:11).

As difficult and troubling as the doctrine of eternal punishment may be, we must not try to make the Bible say what we want it to say. John Walvoord writes, "The doctrine of eternal punishment, though unpopular with liberal scholars and difficult to accept, is nevertheless clearly taught in the Bible."[2]

Finally, the voice from heaven promises blessings and rewards to those saints who persevere to the point of death during this horrific time. They "may rest from their labors, for their deeds follow with them" (Revelation 14:13).

How does each of these four announcements highlight God's power over all events on earth and the destinies of both the wicked and the righteous?

_____

_____

_____

How do you think the believers in the first century who were suffering from persecution would respond to these announcements?

_____

_____

_____

STARTING YOUR JOURNEY

Throughout this preview of coming attractions, God reminds us that He's in control and that His victory is assured. Long before these events come to pass, the outcome is certain. God takes full responsibility for every detail. He leaves nothing to chance. His plans are comprehensive and unchangeable.

If God will be and do all of these things during the end times, when things appear to be out of control, we can be sure that He is working out all the details of our own lives for our good and His glory.

In Revelation 14:6–7, the "eternal gospel" is pronounced over the whole earth. The details of this gospel are spelled out for us in the New Testament. According to 1 Corinthians 15:1–5, what are the main points of the gospel message?

_____

_____

_____

According to Ephesians 2:8–9, how is a person saved? Fill in the key words below:

"For by _____ you have been saved through _____; and that not of _____, it is the _____ of God; not as a result of _____, so that no one may boast."

Have you been saved by grace through faith in Christ's death and resurrection? If you are unsure about your relationship with God, read the section "How to Begin a Relationship with God" at the end of this book.

Once a person has accepted the good news of Jesus Christ and the free gift of eternal life, he or she can have complete confidence that all things—without exception—will work out for the ultimate good.

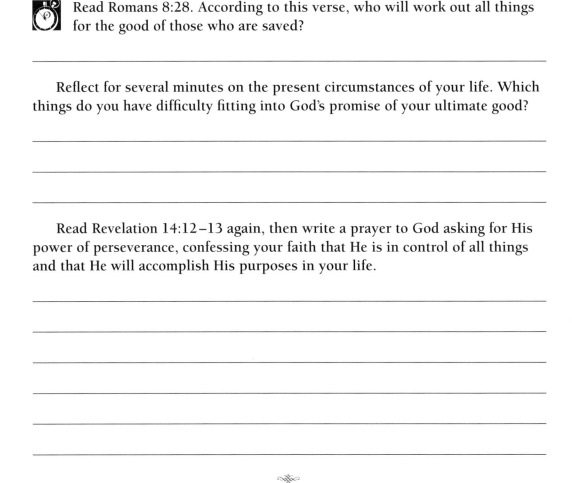 **Read Romans 8:28. According to this verse, who will work out all things for the good of those who are saved?**

_____

Reflect for several minutes on the present circumstances of your life. Which things do you have difficulty fitting into God's promise of your ultimate good?

_____

_____

_____

Read Revelation 14:12–13 again, then write a prayer to God asking for His power of perseverance, confessing your faith that He is in control of all things and that He will accomplish His purposes in your life.

_____

_____

_____

_____

_____

_____

❖

In this lesson we witnessed a preview of coming attractions: the redeemed remnant of Israel standing on Mount Zion and the profound proclamations warning all people of the coming judgment while encouraging believers to persevere. God's sovereign control over all these details means He can make sure pronouncements, even thousands of years before they come to pass. That same God has complete control over the details of our own lives, and we can trust that in His goodness, He will never let us down.

REVELATION

"I am the Alpha . . ." (1:8)   ". . . and the Omega" (22:13)

	"The things which you have seen . . ." Personal and biographical	"The things which are . . ." Christ's letters to the seven churches	"The things which will take place . . ." (Revelation 1:19) Christ as Judge (chaps. 4–5) The Tribulation (chaps. 6–18) The Coming of Christ (chap. 19) The Millennium (chap. 20) The Eternal State (chaps. 21–22)
	CHAPTER 1	*CHAPTERS 2–3*	*CHAPTERS 4–22*
Scope	History: looking back		Prophecy: looking ahead
Style	Dialogue		Observations and questions
Scene	On earth		Shifts between earth and heaven
Main Theme	Christ's future triumph over the forces of evil and His re-creation of the world for the redeemed		
Key Verses	1:7, 19; 22:12–13		

LESSON TWO

GOD'S TERRIBLE, SWIFT SWORD

Revelation 14:14–20

THE HEART OF THE MATTER

In the closing seven verses of Revelation 14, John described the Lord's final judgment using vivid word pictures that an ancient grower of grain or grapes would appreciate. As we read about the Son of Man swinging His sharp sickle of judgment, we are reminded that God's justice holds us accountable for our choices. We must accept or reject His truth. Whatever our choice, we have been warned.

In preparation for this lesson, read Revelation 14:14–20.

YOU ARE HERE

Jesus. No matter whom you're speaking with, that name elicits a response. Almost every human has heard the name of Jesus and associates an image or an idea with it. Sometimes their impressions conform to the Bible; other times they land far from the source, replacing the real Jesus with false concepts.

How do you think people from other religions would describe Jesus? List several words they might use to describe Him.

_____

_____

_____

_____

Compare and contrast these ideas with what the Bible says about Jesus. What, if anything, is different? What is inaccurate?

_____

_____

_____

_____

Do you think most people generally view Jesus as a meek, mild, suffering teacher and servant or as a powerful, majestic, wrathful judge and king? Explain your answer.

_____

_____

_____

_____

The hour fast approaches when Jesus Christ will return from heaven with power and great glory. All the misconceptions about who Jesus was and is will be dispelled in a moment, and the whole world will be forced to face the full biblical truth about Christ, the Savior who not only died for our sin but is also coming again to judge the living and the dead. We cannot merely emphasize the first coming of Christ as prophet and sacrifice; we must also embrace Him as judge and king.

The Two Comings of Christ: A Study in Contrasts	
At His First Coming . . .	At His Second Coming . . .
He came in meekness as a servant (Matthew 20:28).	He will come in power as judge (Matthew 24:30–31; 25:31–46; John 5:26–29).
He came in humility and gentleness (Matthew 11:29; John 5:41).	He will come in majesty and splendor (1 Thessalonians 4:16; Revelation 1:7).
He came to seek and save the lost (Matthew 18:11; Luke 19:10; John 3:17).	He will come to judge and reign (Acts 10:40–42; 2 Corinthians 5:10; Revelation 11:15).
He came to suffer for sinners (Matthew 16:21; 17:12; Mark 9:12).	He will come to rescue the righteous (1 Corinthians 15:51–52; 1 Thessalonians 4:15–17).
He came to sow the seed (Matthew 13:3–9; Luke 8:11).	He will come to reap the harvest (Matthew 13:37–42).

 DISCOVERING THE WAY

In Revelation 14:1–13, John gave us a preview of coming events: the gathering of the remnant of Israel on Mount Zion at the physical return of Christ (14:1–5), followed by the worldwide pronouncement of the gospel (14:6), the fall of Babylon (14:8), the warning to those who worship the Beast (14:9), and promises to encourage the Tribulation saints (14:12–13).

The remainder of Revelation 14 describes the final judgments. They are portrayed as two divine harvests of wrath—the grain harvest (14:14–16) and the grape harvest (14:17–20). The first previews the seven bowl judgments that will be described in detail in Revelation 16; the second represents the infamous Battle of Armageddon, described in 16:13–21 and 19:19–21.

THE GRAIN HARVEST: SEVEN BOWL JUDGMENTS (REVELATION 14:14–16)

The metaphor in John's vision would have been very familiar to the agrarian culture of his day. As a field of wheat ripens, a sense of urgency overtakes the farmer. The crop he planted and cultivated demands to be taken in. The day of harvest cannot be put off. In the same sense, the progression of human affairs, begun in Genesis and advanced by God's sovereignty through the millennia, will culminate in the events in Revelation.

Finally, in Revelation 14:15, the voice of the angel declares, "The harvest of the earth is ripe." The term translated "ripe" literally means, "dry, shriveled, withered." [1] Some translations of the Bible render the word as "overripe." The Lord, in His mercy, will delay judgment as long as possible, but the day of harvest will arrive.

In this vision, John described a luminous white cloud on which "one like a son of man" sits (Revelation 14:14). While the identity of the person is not explicitly stated, the use of imagery and allusion to other Scripture identifies Him for us.

Read Daniel 7:13–14. Who was this Old Testament prophet describing?

_____

Read Matthew 24:30–31. What terms and images do you find in common with Revelation 14:14?

_____

_____

_____

 DIGGING DEEPER
Why Is the Son of God Called the Son of Man?
The expression "Son of Man" in Revelation 14:14 is used to refer to Christ for two important purposes. First, this Hebrew idiom was often used to emphasize the *humanity* of the person referenced. For instance, Daniel found himself trembling in the presence of angels, who referred to him as a "son of man" (Daniel 8:17). Similarly, Jesus often used "Son of Man" to highlight His human qualities—the frailty and limitations of the human body—which existed in union with His divinity (Matthew 8:20; 12:40; 17:12; John 3:14; 8:28).

Second, the title "Son of Man" calls attention to God's participation in our suffering by becoming a human being in the person of Jesus Christ, the

God-man. According to Hebrews 4:15, we have a High Priest who understands our struggles, having endured the full brunt of Satan's temptations. Because Jesus did not sin, He is qualified to represent us before God the Father. And because He has experienced our difficulty, we have confidence in His sympathy.

God needs no qualification to judge us other than His authority as Creator, yet His experience as a Son of Man leaves us with no room to accuse Him of bias. How appropriate that our sympathetic High Priest should be our Judge as well!

Wearing the victor's crown and wielding a sickle, the Son of Man responds to the word of the Father through the angel (see John 5:28–30; 8:28–29): "Put in your sickle and reap!" (Revelation 14:15). Commentator Robert Thomas wrote of Revelation 14:16, "The brevity of the statement dramatizes the suddenness of the judgment."[2] Like an overripe wheat field demands quick and decisive action, the evil of mankind will call for swift justice.

THE GRAPE HARVEST: ARMAGEDDON JUDGMENT (REVELATION 14:17–20)

While the wheat harvest illustrates the speed and totality of the Lord's intervention in human affairs, the grape harvest depicts the severity of His judgment. This vision draws upon another scene that would have been very common in the ancient world. Grapes are thrown into a winepress—a large, bathtub-shaped vat carved into the rock and connected to a lower receptacle via a narrow channel. As the clusters of grapes are crushed underfoot in the upper chamber, the juice flows down the channel into the lower.

In this passage, the grapes are the people who gather to bring war against the Lord in the valley of Har-Megiddo (better known by its more common spelling, Armageddon), and the juice is their mingled blood.

In Revelation 14:17, John described another angel who wields a sickle like the Lord of the wheat harvest.

Read Revelation 6:9–10 and 8:3–4. How are the prayers of the saints and the command of the angel in Revelation 14:18 related?

_____

_____

_____

Like the harvest of wheat, the harvest of grapes is sudden, swift, and total. In one swing, the people of the earth will be gathered and thrown into the vat of the winepress.

The word used in Revelation 14:18 for "ripe" differs from the word that described the wheat harvest. This term means to be fully grown or "to be at the prime."[3] In the delicate art of wine making, the timing of the harvest is a crucial factor in producing excellent wine. Expert winemakers keep a close watch on the vines, waiting for the precise day to cut the clusters and crush them for juice. Similarly, the timing of the great Armageddon judgment will be perfect.

Read Joel 3:12–14 and Isaiah 63:1–4. Describe the similarities you see between these Old Testament prophecies and Revelation 14:17–20.

_____

_____

_____

_____

The grape harvest and the winepress foreshadow the battle of Armageddon described in Revelation 16:14–16 and 19:11–15. The nations of the earth will gather in defense and defiance against the Lord; however, nothing will keep Him from recapturing the earth from the forces of Satan. And the slaughter will be staggering. One expositor writes, "Armageddon, as this passage indicates, will actually be a slaughter rather than a battle. . . . While the angel cuts the grapes, it is the Lord Jesus Christ who crushes out their lives."[4]

STARTING YOUR JOURNEY

Many choose to nurture a cozy image of Jesus as the meek and mild suffering servant, which allows them to reject the Lord's call for submission. Much of the New Testament describes a gentle Jesus, yet we also see that He is a powerful king and a severe judge. The course of human events will eventually demand His judgment, which will be timely, swift, complete, and appalling.

As we peer into the future and consider the complete Jesus—both the gentle priest and the severe judge—two principles present themselves.

First, *God's justice holds every person accountable.* In Genesis 2:15–17, God taught humanity its first lesson: with the gift of choice comes accountability. The choice to sin will reap consequences; the penalty for sin is death (Romans 6:23).

Describe your thoughts and emotions when you see Jesus described as a warrior and a judge in Revelation and other passages.

_____

_____

_____

How does the image of Jesus crushing rebellious people beneath His feet affect your view of Him? How should this affect your devotional life (prayer, Scripture reading, meditation, and so on)?

_____

_____

_____

Second, *God's grace grants every person the freedom to refuse His gift.* Imagine two enormous armies preparing for combat on opposite sides of a vast valley. On one side stands an army of rebellious men and women, led by Satan and dedicated to the destruction of the Lord and His kingdom. On the other stands the army of God, led by Jesus Christ.

When you were born, you were automatically enlisted and counted among the ranks of the evil army. The day of battle will soon arrive. Both sides wait and prepare for attack, but in the meantime you hear an amplified voice from across the valley offering the invitation, *Leave the evil army, cross the battle line, join the ranks of Christ, and you will live.* No one on earth will force you to accept the invitation. You answer only to God.

Revelation 19:14 and 19:19 describe two distinct groups. With which army have you enlisted? How do you know?

_____

_____

_____

If you are uncertain about how to cross this valley and enlist in God's army, read "How to Begin a Relationship with God" located at the back of this book.

The battle lines have been drawn and the ranks of both armies are mounting now. Each of us is presently camped on one side or the other. Unless we have answered the invitation, the winepress awaits us.

> *Mine eyes have seen the glory of the coming of the Lord,*
> *He is trampling out the vintage where the grapes of wrath are stored;*
> *He hath loosed the fateful lightning of His terrible swift sword—*
> *His truth is marching on.*
>
> *He has sounded forth the trumpet that shall never sound retreat,*
> *He is sifting out the hearts of men before this judgment seat;*
> *O be swift, my soul, to answer Him! be jubilant, my feet!*
> *Our God is marching on.*[5]

LESSON THREE

THE ORIGINAL TEMPLE OF DOOM

Revelation 15:1–8

THE HEART OF THE MATTER
We've encountered the seven seal judgments, followed by the blowing of the seven trumpet judgments. Ultimately, the seven bowl judgments will be poured out, climaxing in the battle of Armageddon (Revelation 16:14–16). In this lesson, Revelation 15 provides a prelude to the bowl judgments as it records a remarkable contrast between the triumphant, surviving saints singing their "song of the Lamb" (15:3) and seven powerful angels holding "bowls full of the wrath of God" to pour out on the earth (15:7).

In preparation for this lesson, read Revelation 15:1–8.

YOU ARE HERE
During the 1970s, dirty, disheveled prophets of doom could be seen on the street corners of most major cities in America. They wore sandwich boards that read: *REPENT! THE END IS NEAR!* While most passersby dismissed them as kooks, their signs reflected a shared uneasiness as international upheaval cast a pall over the decade. But more significantly, the bold warning reminded readers then, as it would today, of an uncomfortable truth:

WE FACE IMMINENT JUDGMENT . . . AND WE ARE GUILTY!

Indeed, the Bible declares, "All have sinned and fall short of the glory of God" (Romans 3:23) and "People are appointed to die once, and then to face judgment" (Hebrews 9:27 NET).

21

Briefly describe a time when your performance, knowledge, or skills were evaluated by someone in authority.

_____

_____

_____

_____

_____

Imagine going into such a meeting knowing that you fall far short of the minimum standard. Describe how you might feel.

_____

_____

_____

_____

_____

What one word best describes this attitude or feeling?

_____

DISCOVERING THE WAY

A significant portion of John's revelation describes the coming judgment of God on humankind. This judgment has been divided into three groups of seven events, beginning with seven seals (Revelation 6:1–8:6), followed by seven trumpets (Revelation 8:7–9:21), and concluding with seven bowls (Revelation 16:1–21). Chapters 12–15 provide an interlude between the seven trumpets and the seven bowls. The initial verses of Revelation 15 involve two contrasting scenes: joy in heaven (15:1–4) and dread on earth (15:5–8).

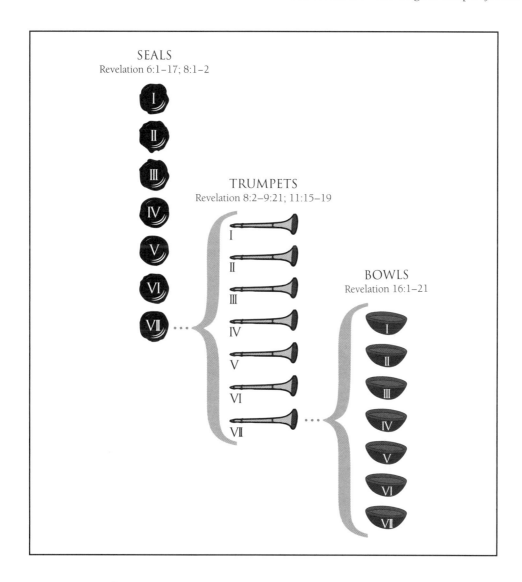

JOY IN HEAVEN (REVELATION 15:1–4)

"Then I saw another sign" (Revelation 15:1) marks the beginning of a new vision, a prelude to the bowl judgments detailed in Revelation 16. From 15:1, we learn two important facts.

First, the bowls represent seven worldwide plagues. The word translated "plague" means, literally, a "blow" or "wound." [1] It's taken from a verb meaning "to strike." [2] These judgments are not long, drawn-out famines or epidemics. Each affliction will be a swift, severe blow.

Second, the seven bowl judgments will be the last expression of God's wrath toward the earth. The battle of Armageddon will be the ultimate, climactic event in the great war between good and evil.

 Read Revelation 15:2–4. Whom does John see in his vision? (Compare Revelation 7:9–17.)

_____

_____

_____

What are they doing?

_____

In Revelation 15:3–4, John referred to "the song of Moses" and "the song of the Lamb," and then he provided a set of lyrics. Commentators offer several theories for the identity of the songs. Most agree that the song of Moses refers to one of two Old Testament passages: Exodus 15:1–18, which Moses composed after the Lord's victory over the Egyptians at the Red Sea; or Deuteronomy 32:1–43, which he composed just as the Israelites were about to enter the Promised Land. Both of these would have been very familiar to New Testament believers.

The song of the Lamb, however, appears to be either new or unfamiliar. So John supplied the lyrics. Both songs praise God for His attributes: who He is, His ways, and what He has done.

One commentator observes:

> The song of Moses was sung at the Red Sea, the song of the Lamb is
> sung at the crystal sea; the song of Moses was a song of triumph over
> Egypt, the song of the Lamb is a song of triumph over Babylon; the

song of Moses told how God brought His people out, the song of the
Lamb tells how God brings His people in; the song of Moses was
the first song in Scripture, the song of the Lamb is the last. The song
of Moses commemorated the execution of the foe, the expectation of
the saints, and the exaltation of the Lord; the song of the Lamb
deals with the same three themes. The song of Moses was sung by a
redeemed people; the song of the Lamb is sung by a raptured people.[3]

Just as important as the words the people are singing is the fact that they are
singing! This is a celebration. During the Great Tribulation, multitudes will come to
know Christ as Savior, resist the Antichrist, and suffer martyrdom for their faith. They
will overcome:

- the Beast and related political pressure to reject Christ

- the false prophet and overt religious pressure to reject Christ

- the number of the Beast and fierce economic pressure to reject Christ
  (Revelation 13)

Then, on the eve of their tormentors' judgment, the Tribulation saints will gather
for worship and thanksgiving. A song of praise will replace their previous anguished
cries for justice (Revelation 6:9–11).

**Considering the lyrics of the song in Revelation 15:3–4, why do you
think the people are joyful?**

_____

_____

_____

DREAD ON EARTH (REVELATION 15:5–8)

As John listened to the vast choir of Tribulation saints, something stole his attention.
Preparations were being made for the final outpouring of God's wrath on the world
(Revelation 15:5–8). We see that, while the believers rejoice in heaven, those who
have rejected the Lord's free offer of eternal life will suffer horrific judgment.

In order to help John understand the events taking place in heaven, the Lord gave John familiar symbols. This vision included a temple, similar to the physical building that had once stood in Jerusalem. (By the time of John's writing, it had been completely destroyed in AD 70.) In contrast to the earthly temple, this figurative temple in heaven had at least one important difference. Nothing concealed the "most holy place" or the "holy of holies"—the sacred place where the presence of the Lord appeared. This area was closed in the earthly temple (Leviticus 16:2–3; Hebrews 9:2–7). Only the high priest could enter once a year to make sacrifices for the people. Sinful humanity could not stand in the presence of the Holy One without suffering the immediate consequence of sin: death.

The earthly temple was built for the very purpose of inviting people into a personal relationship with God. In heaven, where no sin exists, the temple of the Holy One stands wide open. For those who worship, nothing obscures His glory. But for those who rebel, it is a symbol of doom.

As the vision unfolds, seven angels emerge from the heavenly temple, each clothed in the symbol of purity—white linen—and adorned like Christ (Revelation 1:13). They approach the four living creatures (Revelation 4:5–11; 5:6–8; 6:1–8) who give each of them a bowl filled with the wrath of God. These bowls may be connected with the bowls filled with the prayers for vindication offered by the martyred believers in Revelation 5:8, only these bowls "do not exhale the smoke of gratefulness to God, but are full of poisonous, hot, bitter wine, from which emanates the divine majesty whose intense holiness breaks forth in judgment against human sin."[4] These bowls of plagues will be poured out onto the earth.

GETTING TO THE ROOT

The Greek word translated as "bowl" refers to a shallow, saucer-like dish used to boil liquids as well as for "drinking or pouring libations."[5] One dictionary adds that the use of this term in Revelation is "suggestive of rapidity in the emptying of the contents."[6] The dish will splash the earth with the boiling hot wrath of God.

A STUDY IN CONTRASTS

John's preliminary vision before the pouring out of the seven plagues underscores three important contrasts.

As the temple fills with God's glory . . .	. . . the earth is filled with His wrath.
In days past, the wrath of God poured out on Christ for what He did for sinners . . .	. . . in days future, the wrath of God will pour out on sinners for what they did to Christ.
While the believers in heaven rejoice over the triumph of good . . .	. . . the rebellious on earth suffer with the destruction of evil.

The imminence of the bowl judgments should fill the unbeliever with fear and dread, hopefully to the point of repentance. Even as the bowls are poured out, the invitation to believe and be saved stands. Those who have placed their faith in Jesus Christ for eternal life should experience a sobering sense of vindication. At long last, the earth, groaning under the oppression of evil, will finally see the permanent triumph of good (Romans 8:20–22).

STARTING YOUR JOURNEY

A. W. Tozer wrote, "We talk of [God] much and loudly, but we secretly think of Him as being absent, and we think of ourselves as inhabiting a parenthetic interval between the God who was and the God who will be. And we are lonely with an ancient and cosmic loneliness."[7] John's vision of the triumph of good over evil gives future events a present significance. His contrasting visions of joy in heaven and sorrow on earth suggest at least two appropriate responses for us today:

First, we should express *gratitude for God's promise of protection*.

At the beginning of this lesson, you were asked to describe your reaction to having your performance, knowledge, or skills evaluated by someone in authority. Imagine now that this evaluation will depend not upon your own merits but upon those of a renowned expert instead. How would you feel as the appointment drew closer?

_____

_____

_____

What one word best describes your feeling or attitude?

_____

Prior to the Tribulation events described in Revelation 15, those people on earth who have placed their faith in Jesus Christ will be "caught up together with them [resurrected believers who have died before] in the clouds to meet the Lord in the air" (1 Thessalonians 4:17). While the final triumph of good over evil is yet future, believers in Christ can rest in and offer thanks for victory over the enemy and God's provision of a secure place in His love.

Take a few moments to write a brief prayer of thanksgiving for the Lord's promise of safety, both now and in the future.

_____

_____

_____

_____

_____

Our second response should be *concern for those who choose to reject Christ.*

After the church is raptured (1 Thessalonians 4:16–17) and the Antichrist rises to power, fully subjecting the world to evil, some will realize that their choice to reject Christ was a tragic error and will turn to Him. Many others will renounce Jesus as their sovereign Lord and experience horrible suffering as a result.

The most important decision in life is the choice to accept God's promise of protection in His Son, Christ. Therefore the greatest concern for believers must be lost loved ones.

In the space below, write the initials of someone you know to be particularly insensitive to spiritual matters or especially hardened against God.

_____

Describe what you see as his or her greatest challenge to belief in Christ.

_____

_____

_____

Effective evangelism *always* begins with earnest prayer. Before doing anything else, pray; then move only as the Lord brings clarity to your mind. In the space below, write an initial prayer for the person you listed and then for yourself as you two interact in the future.

_____

_____

_____

_____

_____

_____

_____

_____

_____

_____

_____

_____

_____

_____

_____

_____

_____

_____

_____

❧

In the 1970s most people dismissed the grim street corner prophets of doom, though their message was more timely and accurate than any wanted to admit. Judgment is an unsettling prospect—unless you're prepared. Believers can rejoice when Jesus invades the earth and calls evil into account. Those who have trusted Christ can look forward to that day with great anticipation and thanksgiving as we anticipate the song of the Tribulation saints, "For all the nations will come and worship before You, for Your righteous acts have been revealed" (Revelation 15:4).

LESSON FOUR

THE FINAL SEVEN SUPER BOWLS

Revelation 16

THE HEART OF THE MATTER

Revelation 16 describes seven bowl judgments that culminate in the battle of Armageddon (16:16). These last seven judgments are the worst of all—we could call them the "super bowls of judgment." In the events leading up to the final, cataclysmic clash between Christ and Satan, we see the inevitability of the Lord's victory and the progressive, methodical nature of His wrath. Even as He carries out justice, He provides ample opportunity for repentance. But those who suffer through the plagues refuse to repent.

In preparation for this lesson, read Revelation 16:1–12, 17–21.

YOU ARE HERE

However good our intentions, some people insist upon being our ene-mies. The pain they cause can be devastating. Enemies set out to cause harm, either out of hatred for us or love for themselves. Nevertheless, Jesus said, "Love your enemies, do good to those who hate you, bless those who curse you, pray for those who mistreat you" (Luke 6:27–28). Those short, simple com-mands are reasonable and wise in theory, but they can be terribly difficult to apply in real life. Jesus wants us to return good for evil, even as we nurse the wounds caused by our enemies' most recent attacks. Furthermore, this world—twisted by sin and dominated by evil—rewards the deeds of those who mistreat the innocent.

Let's face it; our enemies often seem to have the advantage. The temptation to gain a little justice for ourselves can be overwhelming at times. Yet the words of our Lord resonate with the voice of the Spirit within us, "Love your enemies, do good to those who hate you, bless those who curse you, pray for those who mistreat you."

Describe a time when a nonbeliever caused you personal harm. How did you feel about him or her?

_____

_____

_____

How did this experience affect your relationship with the Lord and your confidence in the value of doing what is right?

_____

_____

_____

If we are honest, we must admit that leading a life that is pleasing to Christ can be perplexing when viewed from a temporal perspective. The present world system punishes rather than rewards Christlike behavior. That can be demoralizing for us over time. Jesus had the advantage of a viewpoint that extended beyond His circumstances. He lived and taught with an eternal, cosmic point of view. To make our obedience less difficult, He shared His eternal perspective with us through the apostle John and the Apocalypse.

DISCOVERING THE WAY

Revelation 16 describes the final round of ever-increasing judgments on the people who stubbornly take the side of evil against the Lord. You may notice some similarities between these bowl judgments and those announced by the seven trumpets.

As we study this last, frightful set of seven judgments, take note of two important observations.

First, God's judgment will not come as one sudden, catastrophic end of all life, but as many judgments, allowing ample opportunity for repentance.

Second, the judgments will grow progressively more severe, providing greater impetus to submit to the Lord before He puts an end to all evil.

First Four Super Bowls of Judgment: The Natural Realm (Revelation 16:1–9)

The first four bowl judgments, like the first four seal and trumpet judgments, form a cluster. Directed against the natural world, their purpose is to seize the attention of all people and prepare them to understand the purpose of the supernatural afflictions that will follow.

Complete the following chart, comparing the events that accompany each bowl. Note the means by which each judgment is delivered, where each judgment is targeted, and the results of each judgment.

	First Bowl (16:2)	Second Bowl (16:3)	Third Bowl (16:4–7)	Fourth Bowl (16:8–9)
Means	*A malignant sore*			
Target				
Results				

These afflictions are reminiscent of the first four trumpet judgments described in Revelation 8:7–13, only more extensive and more intense. In some cases, the plagues are specifically targeted to affect only people who have chosen to align themselves with the Antichrist's government, recalling the plagues that fell upon the Egyptians during the Exodus of Israel (Exodus 8:21–23; 9:2–6; 10:22–23; 11:4–7).

Each plague should come as no surprise. Everyone who will be afflicted by the plagues will have had access to the same predictions you are studying now. Furthermore, each successive scourge builds upon the prophecies fulfilled just a short time before. Humanity will have no excuse for continued rebellion.

Revelation 16:9 summarizes the effect of the plagues carried out in the natural realm. How will the people respond? In your own words or using a dictionary, define what it means to "blaspheme."

_____

_____

_____

John uses the Greek word rendered "blaspheme" in only one other context—when describing the activities and characteristics of the Beast (Revelation 13:4–6; 17:3). **What point do you think he was making by using the term in the context of Revelation 16:9?**

_____

_____

_____

NEXT TWO SUPER BOWLS OF JUDGMENT: THE RULER'S DOMAIN (REVELATION 16:10–16)

As with the trumpet judgments, the first four bowls are directed against the natural realm (the earth, the sea, freshwater sources, and the sun). They are disasters of enormous proportions, but natural nonetheless. The fifth and sixth bowl judgments are supernatural, like the fifth and sixth trumpets, which makes them difficult to describe or imagine.

🕐 Compare the fifth trumpet (9:1–11) with the fifth bowl (16:10–11). What terms and images do you see in common?

_____

_____

_____

_____

Who or what was the target of the fifth trumpet plague (9:4) and the fifth bowl judgment (16:10)?

_____

_____

The book of Revelation offers very little detail about the fifth bowl, describing only darkness and pain for those who swear allegiance to the Beast's kingdom. John often used the image of light to speak of life in the Spirit, and he used darkness as a metaphor for the world's system, which is opposed to the kingdom of God. This affliction is most likely a deepening of the darkness brought on by the fifth trumpet, and it is reminiscent of the plague of darkness that God brought on Egypt (Exodus 10:21–23).

Revelation 16:11 reminds us that the afflictions suffered by the enemies of God are cumulative. The sores brought on by the first bowl continue to fester as the darkness closes in around them. The water that would have soothed their sun-scorched flesh now stands in stinking pools; once-clean water is polluted with decaying blood. Nevertheless, the people refuse to repent. In fact, they only grow more rebellious, which prompts the pouring of the sixth bowl (Revelation 16:12).

🕐 The sixth bowl differs from all the seal judgments, trumpet judgments, and the previous five bowls. How?

_____

_____

_____

_____

John reveals that the "kings from the east" and all the armies of the world will rally for war at a place called "Armageddon" (Revelation 16:13–16). This is a Greek transliteration of the Hebrew term, *Har-Megiddo*, which means "the mountain of Megiddo," or "the hill country of Megiddo." The next lesson will examine Revelation 16:12–16 more closely, focusing on the events that will occur at Armageddon.

DOORWAY TO HISTORY
Holy Land, Holy War

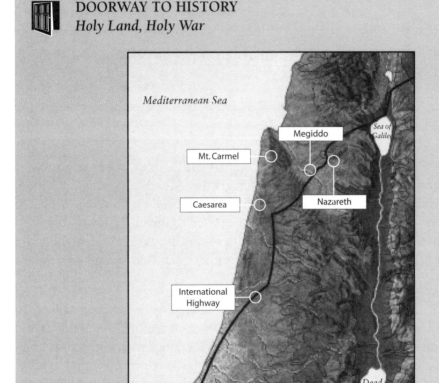

Like any boy growing up in Nazareth, Jesus would have known the local geography and the historical significance of the hills that surrounded His city. The southern ridge of the town, today called the Nazareth Ridge, overlooks the vast Jezreel valley, the site of countless clashes between the world's greatest armies. If He squinted His eyes, He could peer across the valley and just make out the town of Megiddo, well known as the most militarily strategic city in the Middle East.

The international highway that carried troops and commerce from Mesopotamia to Egypt ran the full length of Israel, meandering through the Mount Carmel mountain range. Megiddo guarded the entrance to the most important pass through the ridge. Pharaoh Thutmose III, who fought the Canaanites in 1468 BC, saw the importance of the stronghold and declared, "It is the capture of a thousand cities, this capture of Megiddo."[2]

Megiddo's geographic "location has throughout history made direct control a matter of singular strategic importance, from the armies of [Pharaoh] Thutmose III in the fifteenth century BC to General Allenby's in World War I."[3] Archaeologists have uncovered no less than twenty distinct strata of civilization, each one recognizing the supreme value of its location.

For as long as anyone can remember, Megiddo and the surrounding hill country has been a place of war. As the young Jesus anticipated His earthly ministry, He likely knew that one day Megiddo would be the rallying point for the armies of the Antichrist. There, those who would gather to defy His sovereign rule will suffer judgment for their rebellion.

Perhaps foreseeing the slaughter of Armageddon fueled His compassion for those who did not know Him as Messiah. Perhaps seeing their end gave Him the ability to look down from the cross and say, "Father, forgive them; for they do not know what they are doing" (Luke 23:34).

LAST SUPER BOWL OF JUDGMENT: THE ENTIRE WORLD (REVELATION 16:17–21)

As the kingdoms of the earth gather to fight in the expansive Jezreel valley, the seventh angel will splash out the contents of the final bowl.

In Revelation 16:17, the form of the verb translated as "done" stresses the present effect of a past event, indicating that "the judgment of God has already occurred, and we are at the end of history. The meaning of [this verb] is related to its meaning 'happen' or 'come to pass.'"[4] In other words, this cataclysmic end of the world and the evil that corrupted it was ordained long ago, predicted many times through history, and with the pouring of the seventh bowl will be accomplished.

The description that follows in the remainder of Revelation 16 is a summary account of what John will detail in Revelation 17:1–22:5. What he describes in short order is nothing less than chilling if we read his words using our imaginations.

Have you ever experienced a natural disaster? Perhaps a tornado, hailstorm, or earthquake? What was the experience like? Describe your emotions.

_____

_____

_____

After reading the description of the seventh bowl judgment in Revelation 16:17–20, make a list of the catastrophic events you see described.

_____

_____

_____

For a moment, put yourself into the shoes of those who will experience this final judgment. How would you feel and respond? According to Revelation 16:21, how did people react to these events?

_____

_____

_____

_____

_____

_____

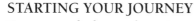

STARTING YOUR JOURNEY

Rest assured, those who mistreat the innocent and choose evil over good will be brought into account. And they will face judgment without excuse. God has announced that the present world system, one that rewards evil and punishes good, will come to a certain and tragic end. John's warning can be distilled into two key truths to remember:

First, *escaping the reality of God's judgment is impossible.*

The psalmist lamented,

> Take a good look! This is what the wicked are like, those who always have it so easy and get richer and richer. I concluded, "Surely in vain I have kept my motives pure and maintained a pure lifestyle. I suffer all day long, and am punished every morning. . . ." When I tried to make sense of this, it was troubling to me. Then I entered the precincts of God's temple, and understood the destiny of the wicked. (Psalm 73:12–14, 16–17 NET)

Second, *remember that postponing repentance is regrettable.*

End-times events could begin at any time—only God knows the exact day and the hour (Revelation 16:15). Those who have hurt you have postponed repentance and face a horrific destiny.

Recall the unbeliever who deliberately caused you or others harm, and then skim over Revelation 16:2–21. Describe how this passage of Scripture influences your attitude toward this person or these people.

_____

_____

_____

Are the horrors of their potential fate enough to ease your anger? How does this perspective affect your desire to see this person or group believe in Jesus Christ?

_____

_____

_____

What are you willing to endure, risk, or sacrifice in order to see this person or these people spared inevitable and terrible judgment?

_____

_____

_____

As Jesus looked down from the cross, He saw His tormentors' destiny, which prompted a prayer interceding for their forgiveness. If we genuinely call Him Lord, we must follow His example.

By the time of Armageddon in the seventh bowl of judgment, humankind will have experienced no less than twenty predicted afflictions, each one more severe than the last, and all of them leading to the final judgment. The Lord could have destroyed the world without warning, but He held off the inevitable judgment in order to give all people opportunity to repent and turn to Him for salvation. Even in His administration of justice, the grace of God abounds!

LESSON FIVE

SHOCK AND AWE REVISITED

Revelation 16:12–16

THE HEART OF THE MATTER

In this lesson, we revisit the final verses of Revelation 16 in order to gain a better understanding of the word *Armageddon*, its place in John's Apocalypse, and the events that will lead to evil's last, desperate attempt to prevent the Lord from taking His rightful place on the throne of the world. A closer look at this section of Scripture is important because the popular media and certain unscrupulous religious figures sometimes twist John's revelation to suit their own purposes.

In preparation for this lesson, read Revelation 16:12–16.

YOU ARE HERE

At the time of this printing, a popular online bookstore returned the following results based on a search of the term *Armageddon*:

> Books – 760
> Music – 173
> Movies – 111
> Home & Garden – 50
> Computer Games & Software – 27
> Apparel – 5
> Miscellaneous – 4

Home & Garden? Needless to say, the word is everywhere. With such intense, ongoing exposure to the perspective of popular media, how accurate is our picture of the event when compared to the way God reveals it in Scripture?

When you hear the word *Armageddon*, what ideas and images immediately come to mind?

_____

_____

_____

What books, movies, or television programs have you seen use the term?

_____

_____

_____

Which has been the most popular or influential? In it, what crisis does the earth face and how is it resolved?

_____

_____

_____

How do you think the images associated with Armageddon in the media affect the perspective of audiences on the future of humankind and on our relationship with God?

_____

_____

_____

_____

_____

DISCOVERING THE WAY

This particular section of Scripture (Revelation 16:12–16) can be especially difficult to interpret correctly. One reliable commentary notes that just the phrase, "the kings from the east," has generated no less than fifty different speculations, "with many expositors trying to relate them to some contemporary leaders of their generation."[1] The interpretation of Revelation, and this section especially, is difficult for at least three reasons.

First, John described an event of such extraordinary significance and immense proportions that words fail to fully capture its magnitude.

Second, John wrote of experiences far removed from his time and culture, and yet he had to express them in a way that any society, in any age, would find accessible and relevant.

Third, John wrote of future events to provide adequate warning so that all people would know how to obey. He did not write merely to predict the future. Therefore, it's important to recognize that the details are important but not vital to his purpose.

Our responsibility as students of the Bible is to examine the text in order to discover principles for living, which may mean accepting that we will not fully understand every image and every nuance. But even if we may not understand all the details, we have enough of the big picture to obey as we should.

WHAT IS ARMAGEDDON? (REVELATION 16:13–16)

At the end of a period of supernatural, extraordinary Tribulation, the military forces of the entire world will gather for war at a place called *Armageddon* in Greek or *Har-Megiddo* in Hebrew (Revelation 16:16). In this epic clash, the armies of the world will be utterly destroyed by Christ at the time of His return to establish His kingdom (see Revelation 19:11–21; we'll explore this further in lesson eight). John's description of the sixth bowl depicts how world events will prepare the enemies of God for destruction. His portrayal involves five elements: an angel, a river, a coalition of kings, an unholy trinity, and a great war.

Read Revelation 16:12–16. Summarize the events of each verse in one or two words. Observe the verses carefully so that you include only what the text says, and leave out any details or clarification it does not provide.

16:12_____

16:13_____

16:14_____

16:15_____

16:16_____

As we saw in the previous lesson, the results of this plague differed greatly from the others. The result of the sixth bowl would seem to favor "the kings from the east." Each of the prior nineteen judgments (seals, trumpets, and bowls) resulted in excruciating pain for those who didn't turn to the Lord for protection. But "God's drying up of the Euphrates is not an act of kindness toward the kings from the east, but one of judgment. . . . [It] will lead them to their doom."[2]

DOORWAY TO HISTORY
The Great River

The Euphrates River is one of the first geographical features mentioned in the Bible. It has been an integral part of world affairs since Creation. It was one of four rivers that irrigated the Garden of Eden before its destruction (Genesis 2:14), and it was supposed to have been the northern and eastern boundaries of the land God promised to Abraham's descendants (Genesis 15:18).

The Hebrews simply called it "the river," or "the great river." The Greeks called it "Euphrates," which means literally, "sweet water."[3] The land between the Euphrates and Tigris rivers, a region the Greeks named "Mesopotamia," gave rise to some of the world's oldest civilizations and greatest empires (including Nebuchadnezzar's Babylon, which John uses to typify the world's system in the book of Revelation).

The Euphrates River divides two stereotypical empires: Babylon on the east and Israel on the west. Of course, at the time of the sixth bowl, the Beast occupies Jerusalem as the world's ruler (Revelation 11:1–2).

Jump ahead to Revelation 16:14 for a moment. According to this verse, who else gathers together?

_____

For what purpose do the kings of the world gather?

_____

_____

_____

We may not know all the specific details, but we know that the sixth bowl judgment allows nations from around the world to gather for war in the Middle East. This will be an unparalleled coalition of armed forces from around the globe.

Returning to Revelation 16:13, what three beings are named? List them in order, then identify each of them based on the Scripture references provided.

Entity	Reference	Identity
	Revelation 12:7–9	
	Revelation 13:1–4	
	Revelation 13:11–17	

Some expositors have called this the "unholy trinity." What do you suppose are some reasons for this?

_____

_____

_____

John didn't explain what the "spirits of demons" will say, what motivates the nations to gather for war, or even who they gather to fight against (Revelation 16:13–14). One commentator offers a reasonable possibility:

> Satan, knowing that the second coming of Christ is near, will gather all the military might of the world into the Holy Land to resist the coming of the Son of Man who will return to the Mount of Olives (Zech. 14:4). Though the nations may be deceived in entering into the war in hope of gaining world political power, the satanic purpose is to combat the armies from heaven (introduced in [Revelation] 19) at the second coming of Christ.[4]

 According to Revelation 16:12, who initiates these events?

_____

How does this truth fit with your understanding of God's perfect plan for all end-times events? (For further explanation, see Revelation 17:17).

_____

_____

_____

While the unholy trinity, the rulers, and the armies of the world will act upon their own evil intentions, they will nevertheless behave predictably and remain under the sovereign control of God. While the Lord is never the author of evil, He will allow wicked people to destroy themselves by their own evil (Romans 1:20–32).

So the armies of the world will gather at Armageddon. (See "Doorway to History" in the previous chapter for more information about the town of Megiddo.) The Jezreel valley will become the battleground for what the participating kings and armies expect to be the greatest war in the history of the world. But what follows can hardly be considered a battle.

OBSERVING THE FINAL JUDGMENT (REVELATION 16:17–21)

In the final judgment of the earth, God's creation, corroded by sin, collapses under the weight of its own evil. Mountains fall, valleys fill, islands sink, and human civilization—what's left of it—is shaken to its stone-age foundation.

Upon what did the angel pour the contents of the seventh bowl in Revelation 16:17?

_____

Read Revelation 16:17–21. **After the voice of the Lord declares, "It is done," what cataclysmic events occur? List them below.**

_____

_____

_____

_____

What words and phrases indicate that these events occur worldwide rather than in Israel alone?

_____

_____

_____

_____

What Revelation describes is nothing less than the end of the world as we know it. Everything about the earth, including its topography, is prepared for a new regime: the thousand-year reign of Jesus Christ.

INTERPRETING THE LANGUAGE OF ARMAGEDDON

In the absence of specific explanations within the text of Scripture itself, we are wise to keep our focus on the big picture until history makes the details obvious. Excessive speculation is the stuff of fiction and the playground of religious hucksters. At this point in history, we know only that Satan will elevate and utilize two great world figures to unite all of the world's great military powers near Megiddo in order to prepare for the ultimate world war.

The disasters of Armageddon will not be anything like those we currently experience. The lightning, earthquakes, hail, and other resulting calamities will be thousands of times more severe. And unlike the natural disasters that occur today, these will have a supernatural source. We incorrectly call tornadoes and tidal waves "acts of God." These are merely the physical fallout of a world made evil by the sinful choice of humankind in Genesis 3. God allows them to occur. The calamities resulting from the seventh and final bowl, however, are brought about by the wrath of God—directly, deliberately, and decisively.

STARTING YOUR JOURNEY

As we square our vision of Armageddon with John's, a few popular notions fall away as some more profound truths come into focus. Take note of these four intriguing observations.

First, *the absence of America is surprising*. In most popular depictions of Armageddon, humans are always the good guys, and they always find a way to cheat disaster and keep the world going just as it is. They also tend to feature America with Americans in central roles. However, we see almost nothing that would indicate that the United States plays any significant role, or even exists at all.

The absence of America in world events as described by Revelation is thought-provoking. What do you think this might suggest about the future of the United States?

_____

_____

_____

Second, *the presence of demonic activity is frightening.* Popular media most often represents Armageddon as a disaster of global proportions, but a *natural* one nonetheless. The Armageddon of the Bible will not be a struggle to overcome a natural catastrophe or a battle fought with guns and missiles, though the armies of the world will foolishly arm themselves for one. Instead, the earth will see the reemergence of supernatural evil on a scale like never before.

Based on your study of Revelation 16:12–16, name three specific differences between the biblical portrayal of Armageddon and that of popular media.

_____

_____

_____

_____

_____

Next, *the resurgence of interest in the Bible is encouraging.* While so much of John's vision has been distorted by various depictions in movies, television, and books, we should be encouraged to see a resurging interest today in the events of the latter days. This gives believers greater opportunity to offer the definitive, authoritative source of truth on the subject, the Bible.

Suppose someone says to you, "A giant meteor is heading toward the earth and scientists predict a complete, global obliteration—Armageddon!" How would you respond?

_____

_____

_____

_____

Finally, *the influence of Christ is compelling*. Popular depictions of the end times rarely, if ever, mention God. Nevertheless, He is central to John's vision, especially in the person of Jesus Christ. As we read of the awful world events that take place before His coming in power and judgment, we must never forget that it is all about Him.

How might you steer someone's new fascination for the end times toward the cause of Christ? Be practical and specific in your answer.

_____

_____

_____

_____

_____

_____

The images of Revelation are intended to be provocative, intriguing, emotionally jarring—even frightening. John wants us to keep the Apocalypse close by as a ready reference while the events of history run their course. Like symbols on a roadmap, the images point to a future we have yet to see. Then, as we approach the landmarks of history, clarity will render our imaginations obsolete, and we will arrive prepared for a place we have never seen. In the meantime, we must hold our speculations loosely and cling to the truth:

EVIL WILL BE CALLED INTO ACCOUNT AND DESTROYED BY GOD;

THE WORLD WILL BE DEMOLISHED TO MAKE WAY FOR A NEW CREATION;

AND,

IN THE END, GOD WINS!

LESSON SIX

THE FINAL EXIT OF WORLDWIDE RELIGION

Revelation 17:1–18

THE HEART OF THE MATTER

Humanity is incurably religious. Since humankind's earliest days on earth, people have sought to earn God's favor through various systems of works-based salvation. Therefore, we should not be surprised that the deceptive message of a works-based religion will play a major role in the last days of planet Earth. John's Apocalypse reveals that this false system of belief will become an essential element of Antichrist's final world kingdom as he engineers his military, political, economic, and philosophical empire. As believers today, our task is to seek out any trace of this falsehood—works-based righteousness—in our relationship with the Lord and replace it with the truth. We are saved and sustained solely by grace through faith in Jesus Christ.

To prepare for this lesson, read Revelation 17:1–18.

YOU ARE HERE

The movie *Saint Ralph* tells the tale of a fourteen-year-old boy who lost his father in World War II and whose mother lies in a coma. He becomes convinced that he can earn his mother's survival by trading one miracle for another. Upon hearing that winning the Boston Marathon would be just such a miracle, this becomes his quest. The warped theology of the story is easy to spot because it is so familiar to our sin-twisted nature: one miracle deserves another. We want to believe that if we work hard enough, suffer long enough, and believe purely enough, the Lord will have no choice but to grant us our deepest desires.

Read each of the statements below, and indicate the degree to which they *seem* genuine in your experience. In other words, despite what your common sense tells you, how do your instincts usually respond? Use the following scale to indicate your involuntary reaction:

1 – I never feel this way.

2 – Sometimes, in quiet moments, this thought feels right.

3 – I really don't know.

4 – I generally feel this is right quite often.

5 – I'm convinced that this is correct.

The Lord withholds blessings because I am unfaithful or disobedient.

1	2	3	4	5

When I experience difficult circumstances, it must be because I am not as faithful as the Lord would like me to be.

1	2	3	4	5

If I please the Lord by my actions, He will be more likely to protect me from harm.

1	2	3	4	5

God helps those who help themselves.

1	2	3	4	5

The better I behave, the more God likes me and wants me to be close to Him.

1	2	3	4	5

I am going to heaven after I die because I am a good person.

1	2	3	4	5

DISCOVERING THE WAY

The desire of humankind to achieve salvation on its own merit has deep roots in our history. Before languages and borders divided us, all people lived in one community, a land called Shinar, under the leadership of one king whose name was Nimrod (Genesis 10:9).

THE BEGINNING OF WORKS-BASED RELIGION (GENESIS 11:1–9)

Genesis 11:1–9 contains the first recorded example of organized, works-based false religion.

Read Genesis 11:1–9. According to 11:4, for whom did the people build the city and the tower?

_____

_____

_____

In your own words, what motivated the people to behave as they did?

_____

_____

_____

Why would the Lord consider this attempt to remain unified an act of disobedience? (For further reference, see Genesis 1:28; 9:1, 7.)

DOORWAY TO HISTORY
Balal, Babel, Babylon

The Greek translation of the Old Testament (known as the Septuagint) identifies the region of Shinar as Babylon in Daniel 1:2, Isaiah 11:11, and Zechariah 5:11; the context of those passages makes this association clear. The use of name-play ("*Babel*" with *bālal*) in Genesis 11:9 also lets us know that the people who built the tower that reached into heaven were the early founders of the first great world empire, Babylon. The Hebrew verb *bālal* can be translated as "confused."[1]

The religious pride of the Babylonians is well documented. "Written Babylonian accounts of the building of the city of Babylon refer to its construction in heaven by the gods as a celestial city"[2] as evidenced by an ancient epic known as the *Enuma Elish*. "The Babylonians took great pride in their building; they boasted of their city as not only impregnable, but also as the heavenly city, *bāb-ili* ('the gate of God')."[3]

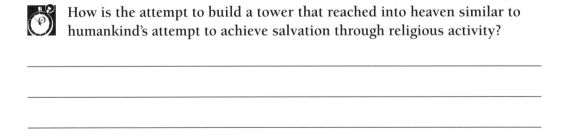

How is the attempt to build a tower that reached into heaven similar to humankind's attempt to achieve salvation through religious activity?

PORTRAYAL OF THE WORLD'S FUTURE SYSTEM (REVELATION 17:1–6, 15)

John used *Babylon* to describe a particular world-oriented system of thinking that is wholly opposed to God's (Revelation 14:8; 18:1–3). Words that characterize Babylon include *pride*, *achievement*, *religiosity*, and *rebellion*.

Read Revelation 17:1–6. What image does this passage use to describe works-based religion ("Babylon the Great")? List several specific characteristics of this metaphor.

_____

_____

_____

_____

_____

_____

According to 17:15, how extensive is her influence?

_____

_____

_____

Who suffers persecution as a result of her seduction of the world in 17:6?

_____

_____

_____

INTERPRETATION OF THE MAJOR EVENTS (REVELATION 17:7–14, 18)

As John stood in utter amazement at the pervasive influence of the harlot, an angel explained the vision's bizarre imagery. Some key phrases and images require explanation based on related passages in Revelation:

Phrase/Image	Scripture	Explanation
many waters	17:1, 15	All people and people groups around the world
the Beast	17:3, 8, 11–14	The Antichrist
seven heads	17:3, 7, 9–10	Seven world empires, five that are in John's past (which some identify as Egypt, Assyria, Babylon, Medo-Persia, and Greece), one that exists in John's present (Rome), and one that is still future (the empire of the Antichrist)
himself also an eighth and is one of the seven	17:11	The Antichrist, who will either fake his own death and resurrection or will do so by the power of Satan in order to amaze the world and win its allegiance
ten horns	17:3, 7, 12	Ten nations who will unite to empower the Antichrist
the great harlot	17:1–8	Works-based religiosity, called "the mother of harlots" because it is the foundation of all false religions, drawing its inspiration from pride, an illusion of self-sufficiency, and a denial of God's grace

ULTIMATE DESTRUCTION OF THE ONE-WORLD RELIGION (REVELATION 17:16–18)

As this particular vision concludes, the Lord reveals an unexpected twist.

 According to Revelation 17:16, who will destroy the harlot?

_____

These earthly forces will, no doubt, believe themselves to be in charge of their own destinies. But who has orchestrated these events (Revelation 17:17)?

_____

How are these events similar to what occurred in Genesis 11:1–9?

_____

_____

_____

With poetic irony, the Antichrist will turn on the false, one-world religious system he helped to formalize and will destroy it. He will eliminate any form of religion that does not hold himself as the sole object of worship. But even this supreme act of treachery against humankind and rebellion against God will serve to achieve the Lord's ultimate plan.

 STARTING YOUR JOURNEY
Our study of Revelation 17 and works-based religion prepares us to reflect on three important principles.

First, *religious activity feels full and alive but is, in truth, empty and dead.* Struggling with the purpose behind religious activity is a normal part of a genuine spiritual life in Christ. While believers become new creatures upon salvation, we do not automatically and immediately start living by the grace that saved us—grace that we received out of God's unconditional love and neither earned nor deserved. As we grow, we often revert to our old, self-sufficient, prideful ways, seeking to earn God's favor on our own only to find that we need Christ as much as ever.

Have you ever engaged in works-based religious activity? It can seem loving or sacrificial on the surface, but these actions are rooted in pride or selfish ambition or in efforts to please other people or earn favor with God. Briefly describe the situation. What was your motivation?

_____

_____

_____

How did you discover it was futile? What damage did it cause?

_____

_____

_____

Read John 15:9–10, Ephesians 2:8–9, and 1 John 3:16–18. What should your motivation for participating in religious activity or service be?

_____

_____

_____

Second, *satanic strategy appears impressive and effective but is, in truth, impotent and deceptive.* Satan, the father of lies, along with his host of demons, has encouraged man in his pursuit of eternal life by means of human effort. He deceives mankind through the lie of self-reliance, seeking to earn God's favor on one's own effort, or through self-condemnation, the lie that one cannot be loved by God. However, God's offer of salvation solely by grace through faith alone immediately cuts off Satan's strategy at the pass.

Let's return for a moment to the first exercise in this lesson. Ask yourself: In the original statement, is there evidence of self-reliance or self-condemnation? Fill in the middle column accordingly. Then carefully read the corrected statement.

False Statement	Self-reliance or Self-condemnation?	True Statement
The Lord withholds blessings because I am unfaithful or disobedient.		The Lord's sole motivation for giving blessings is His grace. He delights to give them, and they cannot be deserved or earned (Luke 11:11–14; Ephesians 3:14–21).
When I experience difficult circumstances, it must be because I am not as faithful as the Lord would like me to be.		Because I live in a world corrupted by sin (Romans 8:20–23), I will experience difficult circumstances, but because of Christ I will never be punished for my sins—not even a little (Romans 8:1, 28).
If I please the Lord by my actions, He will be more likely to protect me from harm.		The Lord has not promised to protect me from harm (James 1:2–4; 1 Peter 4:12–14); nevertheless, He promised that everything will be for my good (Romans 8:28) and that nothing can separate me from Him (Romans 8:38–39).
God helps those who help themselves.		God wants me to rely on Him in all things, rather than on my own strength (Psalm 31:1–3; John 15:3–5). He will provide for my needs.
The better I behave, the more God likes me and wants me to be close to Him.		God loves me and wants me to have an intimate relationship with Him because He created me (Psalm 36:5–9; John 14:1–3; Ephesians 5:25–30, 32; Revelation 21:2–4).
I am going to heaven after I die because I am a good person.		I will go to heaven when I die, not because of anything I do, but because of what Jesus did on my behalf (Romans 5:8; Galatians 2:16; Ephesians 2:8–9).

What will it take for you personally to uncover God's truth about living in grace and begin to believe it instead of the subtle lies in the false statements above? You may wish to talk to a friend or pastor to specifically combat the lies behind your most-believed thought patterns.

_____

_____

_____

Third, *God's sovereignty seems absent and uninvolved but is, in truth, present and active.* A common experience among believers—even the most mature—is the feeling that the Lord remains aloof while evil runs unchecked. It is during these times that we must avoid taking up religious activity in an effort to earn the Lord's favor. It is nothing more than works-based religion—no better than building a tower to heaven in our living room. Nothing we do can ever gain more grace than God already delights to give, and nothing will earn us more favor than His Son has already earned for us on the cross.

When are you most likely to doubt the Lord's sovereignty or involvement?

_____

_____

Give an example of a time when you experienced an awareness of God's sovereignty and His absolute control over events and circumstances? How does this memory boost your faith as you consider countering the works-based activity in your life?

_____

_____

_____

✦

When tempted to work, submit. When troubled with doubt, read His Word. When afflicted by hopelessness, pray that the Lord will allow you to experience the grace He has already given you; then do what doesn't come naturally: wait.

FROM EARTHLY HORRORS TO CELESTIAL HALLELUJAHS

Selections from Revelation 18; 19:1–10

THE HEART OF THE MATTER

After bearing witness to the fall of Babylon in Revelation 18, we will move into chapter 19 to observe the King of kings and Lord of lords as He triumphantly returns to establish Himself as the undisputed Ruler and righteous Judge over the whole earth. At last, we replace all earthly groans, gloom, and doom with a long-awaited series of heavenly hallelujahs! But this end-times change in regime should prompt us not only to rejoice, but to examine where our own attention lies—with the old world that's passing away or with the new world that's coming.

In preparation for this lesson, read Revelation 18:1–19:10.

YOU ARE HERE

What if the entire world as you know it—people, things, events, and activities—were to collapse? What if your sources of comfort, luxury, entertainment, or other enjoyment were lost forever? People say they hope there's _____ in heaven, with the blank filled in with whatever source of earthly joy they happen to enjoy. Others say they hope the Lord will delay His return until they _____, with the blank reflecting the earthly activity or event they value most.

What things would you miss most if they were taken away, lost, or destroyed? Name at least three.

_____

_____

_____

What steps have you taken to protect yourself from losing these things?

_____

_____

_____

In an average week, how much time do you spend gaining, maintaining, or enjoying these things?

_____

_____

_____

If we're really honest with ourselves, we may discover that we are more attached to the things of this world than we care to admit.

 DISCOVERING THE WAY

Revelation 17 and 18 describe a harlot whose sudden rise and fall will be observed by millions. Called "Babylon," she's the mother of evil and all forms of false religion. She represents a lifestyle of enormous wealth and influential power. Of course, Babylon is not a literal woman, but instead the personification of evil in all of its incarnations. As we learned in lesson six, her funeral was announced in Revelation 17. Revelation 18 presents the rebellious world's eulogy. The world's misguided mourning over the fall of Babylon is followed by spontaneous heavenly praise in Revelation 19 as the heavenly bride begins to celebrate the wedding feast of the Lamb.

FAREWELL TO BABYLON (REVELATION 18:1–24)

Though Revelation 17 and 18 provide some significant details about Babylon's religious and commercial power, the big picture resonates in every verse: one day the evil harlot will be utterly destroyed. In the first part of this lesson, we will observe the highlights of her power, which will serve to underscore the end of everything that Babylon represents.

The end of the false religious and political system known as "Babylon" is certain (Revelation 18:1–3). Though her sins were allowed to pile up (18:5), the wrath of God was not forgotten, but stored, as it were, in bowls to be cast down according to God's timing (18:6–8). Yet in the midst of this death sentence, God grants one final opportunity for repentance.

Read Revelation 18:4. If the power and influence of spiritual Babylon during the tribulation period is worldwide, what do you think is meant by "Come out of her, my people"? (See Paul's exhortation in 2 Corinthians 6:14–17.)

_____

_____

_____

 According to the following verses, who are the people that will lament over the fall of Babylon? What are their reasons for mourning?

	Who Laments?	Why?
Revelation 18:9–10		
Revelation 18:11–16		
Revelation 18:17–19		

What specific worldly attachments caused the people to mourn in Revelation 18:9–19?

_____

_____

_____

While John heard loud lamentations pour forth from those who trusted in the last great Babylonian empire, another voice called on those in heaven to rejoice. A vivid word picture follows (Revelation 18:20–21), as an angel demonstrates the violent end that will come to Babylon and all those associated with her. The stone flung into the sea weighed thousands of pounds, and though it created a loud and violent splash, it instantly sunk to the very bottom of the sea.[1]

John Phillips describes the destruction of Babylon in these words: "The pride, the presumption, the perversity of Babylon makes her the final depository of the sins of the world. She was deliberately built to organize, control, and extend the Beast's policies of godlessness, iniquity, oppression, and persecution. Her fall is just."[2]

According to Revelation 18:21–23, what will no longer be found in Babylon?

_____

_____

_____

_____

Most of the things listed are neutral or used positively in the worship and praise of God. What do you think made these particular things so perverse and worthy of judgment when they were done in Babylon?

_____

_____

_____

_____

Do any of these come close to your personal inventory of things you would miss from the present world? If so, which ones?

_____

_____

_____

PRAISE TO YAHWEH (REVELATION 19:1–10)

The classic science-fiction adventure *Star Wars* ended with the dazzling destruction of the Death Star—a moon-sized space station that had terrorized the galaxy as a symbol of evil and tyranny. The epic trilogy *The Lord of the Rings* climaxed with the cataclysmic destruction of the tower of Mordor—a representation of the demonic Dark Lord Sauron's evil oppression. In the same way, the annihilation of Babylon represents the destruction of everything evil and demonic in this present world. And when something so dangerous and despicable is destroyed, God's people rejoice with a joyful chorus of hallelujahs.

That common Old Testament exultation, *hallelujah*, appears four times in this pronouncement of praise (Revelation 19:1, 3, 4, 6). It means "praise the Lord," and surprisingly this is the only place it appears in the entire New Testament. Three groups cry "hallelujah" before God: the saints in heaven (19:1–3), the twenty-four elders (19:4), and the great multitude (19:6). In Revelation 19:1–10, we see at least four reasons for celebration.

First, *they celebrate because the power of God has conquered evil* (Revelation 19:1–2). Often when Christians today speak of "the end of the world," we really mean the end of the unrighteous world system driven by Satan and steered by wicked men and women. The end of that world will be a cause of great rejoicing.

Second, *they celebrate because the Lord God reigns* (Revelation 19:3–6). Until the moment Christ sets foot on this earth and abolishes all earthly rule and authority, God will allow people the freedom to live their own way. But at any moment God could begin to take back the kingdoms of this world. And He will rule through His Son.

Third, *they celebrate because the marriage of the Lamb has come* (Revelation 19:7–8). As the funeral dirge of the wicked fades, the wedding bells of the righteous begin to resound. When the King of kings conquers evil and begins to reign, His bride—the church—will stand at His side and reign with Him. This marriage of Christ and the church elicits great praise and worship of God.

Fourth, *they celebrate because the marriage supper begins* (Revelation 19:9). Just imagine the gathering for that grand supper together! That great banquet will not be about the menu but about the Master.

DOORWAY TO HISTORY
The Bride

The marriage traditions of the ancient Near East were quite different from those of our twenty-first-century Western culture. We can see several distinct stages in the marriage tradition.

The betrothal. The parents sealed a contract and made arrangements for the ceremony, which often took place a year or more later. During this "betrothal" period the man and woman were considered legally married, and a betrothal could only be broken by divorce.

The presentation. During the festivities prior to the actual ceremony, the groom would leave his home and travel to the bride's home, where she would be waiting with her friends. The groom would then claim her as his own beloved bride.

The ceremony. The presentation of the bride would initiate a lengthy time of festivities known as the "wedding supper," which could last several days. The new bride and groom would depart the marriage supper with full rights, privileges, and responsibilities as husband and wife.[3]

The analogy of the church's marriage to Christ reflects these ancient Jewish wedding customs. In God the Father's foresight, He chose the church "before the foundation of the world" (Ephesians 1:4). Then, when sinners are saved they are betrothed to Christ—a binding relationship that still awaits its complete realization. At the presentation, the church will be raptured to meet the Lord in the air (Matthew 25:1–13; 1 Thessalonians 4:17). Then, at the wedding feast of the Lamb, the final consummation will begin as Christ and the church take their places to reign over the earth.[4]

Added to Christ's invitation to the marriage supper we find a clear verification: "These are true words of God" (Revelation 19:9). No exaggeration, no deception, no lies! God said it; He'll do it. And we look forward to that incredible future with Him.

Read Revelation 19:10. Toward what visible, tangible things in this world might you be tempted to direct your worship?

_____

_____

_____

STARTING YOUR JOURNEY

When we consider the great mourning and glorious marriage in Revelation 18:1–19:10, a few practical reminders linger.

First, *remember that our God reigns*. He alone exercises control over all things. The Lord gives us gifts, and the Lord can take them away (Job 1:21). Therefore, stop worrying about things in this world over which you have no ultimate control.

Read Matthew 6:31–34. Do any of these things Jesus warned us about occupy your own thoughts? Which ones?

_____

_____

_____

According to this passage, where should we focus our thoughts, plans, and pursuits?

_____

_____

Second, *remember that only the Lamb is worthy of your worship*. We may not be tempted to worship statues, but all of us struggle with idolatry in different forms: jobs, possessions, people, or talents. God has given these to us as gifts, and we are to worship Christ, the Gift-giver.

Read Matthew 6:19. Have you invested lately in pursuits or possessions that have no eternal value? What will happen to these things when you die or when Christ returns?

_____

_____

_____

Read Matthew 6:24. If an objective observer were to compare the amount of time, energy, and money you spend on your temporal material possessions versus your spiritual life and service of Christ, would he or she say you're a servant of God or a servant of your possessions?

_____

Third, _remember that supper is being served._ You've been invited to the great wedding supper of the Lamb. All you need to do is accept the invitation by faith.

If you've never accepted Christ's invitation, or if you're not sure what that means, read "How to Begin a Relationship with God" at the end of this Bible Companion.

If you have already accepted His invitation, how do you need to prepare for the moment when He will call you up to His great banquet hall? What have you become attached to in this world that may be distracting you from the Bridegroom Himself?

_____

_____

Based on this lesson, what steps can you take this week to refocus your worship on Christ and away from material possessions and the worries of this world? Name specific issues, desires, or objects you need to release and surrender to Him today.

_____

_____

_____

We've all dropped something heavy into a deep body of water, heard the sound of it hitting the surface, and perhaps even felt the splash on our faces. Immediately the object sinks to the bottom—it's gone. In the same way, "Babylon"—the religious, political, and economic world system—will be destroyed, dropped into the abyss, and never heard from again. Worldly values will be sunk forever: lifestyles, sights and sounds, art and architecture—all gone. In light of this reality, are you placing your stock in the spiritual commodities that last . . . or in the earthly things that will pass away with this present world?

LESSON EIGHT

HERE COMES THE KING OF KINGS

Revelation 19:11–21

THE HEART OF THE MATTER

An old saying goes, "The wheels of justice grind slowly, but exceedingly fine." In this passage of Revelation, the grinding comes to an end and justice is accomplished in the dramatic return of the Lord Jesus Christ. Good finally triumphs over evil. Persecution of the righteous finally ends. The schemes of Satan and his demons finally unravel. The political and religious leaders (the Beast and false prophet), who have deceived the world and reduced humankind to its lowest depths of barbarism and violence, finally face their doom. The promise of Christ's triumphant return to earth finally becomes a reality. "The great supper of God" is finally served as the birds fill their stomachs with the flesh of those whom the Conquering King has destroyed at Armageddon. Long-awaited justice rolls down . . . finally. And while that great day is still to come, today we must ask ourselves the question, *Has His kingdom come in my own life?*

In preparation for this lesson, read Revelation 19:11–21.

YOU ARE HERE

The crowds formed early. Long before the Queen was to ride by in her parade carriage, eager subjects and tourists vied for space on the sidewalk near St. James Park in London. As "Trooping the Colour" climaxed with the arrival of the Queen, anyone watching the crowd could easily distinguish between Her Majesty's loyal subjects and mere tourists and bystanders. While British subjects clasped their hands and held their breath, a cynical humor laced the reactions of many Americans, Aussies, and other indifferent onlookers. Obviously the supreme monarch of England holds more weighty significance for some than others, which illustrates an important principle:

What you *are* determines what you *see*,
and what you *see* determines what you *do*!

How would you expect the loyal subjects of King Jesus to behave prior to His arrival?

_____

_____

How might their behavior differ from those who don't know Him personally?

_____

_____

How does the anticipation of Christ's return as Judge and King influence your thinking about evil and the sins people commit against you?

_____

_____

How does it influence your thinking about your own sinful deeds or habits?

_____

_____

DISCOVERING THE WAY

Revelation 19:11–21 describes the dramatic, triumphant arrival of Jesus Christ. This is His second appearance on earth—not to be confused with the Rapture (1 Thessalonians 4:17), during which He will meet His loyal subjects in the clouds and lead them back to heaven to be with Him during the Great Tribulation. In His first appearance, He came as a baby, grew to be a man, announced His identity as King, and offered amnesty to anyone who would believe and be saved (John 3:16–18). In His second appearance, Christ will come as Judge and Supreme Monarch of the world.

THE KING'S ARRIVAL (REVELATION 19:11–16)

John's description of this dramatic entrance never actually names Jesus. However, it provides several unmistakable clues to clearly identify this figure as the Son of God.

The rider of the white horse is identified by three names in Revelation 19:11–16. List them below:

_____ (19:11)

_____ (19:13)

_____ (19:16)

One of these names also appears in John's Gospel (John 1:1–5, 18). How does this name, "The Word of God," fit who Jesus is and what He does?

_____

_____

The rider of Revelation 19 doesn't come to earth alone. Verse 14 tells us that "the armies which are in heaven" follow him on white horses. In addition to the angels, others reside in heaven who may be a part of the Lord's invasion force:

- Raptured believers (Revelation 19:7–8)

- Tribulation believers (Revelation 6:11; 7:13–14)

- Old Testament believers (Daniel 12:1–2)

John described the robes of Christ as blood-soaked. Why? (For a hint, read Revelation 14:19–20 and Isaiah 63:2–4. See "Doorway to History" on the next page.)

_____

_____

_____

What is the significance of this as it relates to Christ's establishing His reign on earth?

_____

_____

_____

 DOORWAY TO HISTORY
The Triumphant Return

John very likely saw in the scene of Christ's return an allusion to the Roman *Triumphus*, the highest honor given to a victorious general returning home. Such ceremonies began with a solemn procession along the *Via Sacra* (Sacred Way) lined with people shouting, "*Lo triumphe.*"[1] In the early days of the empire, a conquering hero rode a white war horse and wore the battle-dress of a Roman general, a red cloak.[2] Over the centuries, however, as the pomp of the ceremony (and the vanity of Rome's victors) grew, the *triumphators* opted for a chariot "drawn, like the chariots of Jupiter and Apollo, by four white horses."[3] Nevertheless, citizens tended to respect a more modest display, saying "Let the other consul drive standing erect in a chariot drawn, if he wished, by many horses. The truly triumphant [way] through the city was on a single horse."[4] The triumphator's children, robed in white, stood with him in the chariot or, more often, rode behind him on trace-horses.[5] His army followed.

As an important rite of the capital, the celebration included every citizen of every rank, and "affirm[ed] the unity and conquering destiny of the state"[6] while officially sharing the spoils of victory. One historian noted: "An observer in Rome, watching the procession pass by, might be pardoned if he thought the Roman people were celebrating the conqueror: in fact they were celebrating themselves. They rejoiced in their victory, incarnate in the figure of the conqueror, and they saw in this earthly procession intimations of divine blessing."[7]

THE BATTLE (REVELATION 19:17–21)

Revelation 19:17–18 begins to describe something that occurs just as the Lord and His army of believers appear in the skies. With the earthly powers of Satan gathered in the plain near Har-Megiddo and the supernatural presence of God and His host assembled in the sky, an angel stands in the sun, in order to command the full attention of the world, and delivers a warning. His "message is gruesome and powerful, guaranteeing before the battle has been joined that the end result is certain. The angel commands all the birds . . . [using] ironically the same verb used in 16:14, 16 for the false trinity 'gathering together' the nations for the final battle. At the same time as the evil forces gather for Armageddon, the carrion birds are called to gather for the aftermath of the inevitable slaughter."[8] Jesus alluded to this during His earthly ministry when He said to His disciples, "For just as the lightning comes from the east and flashes even to the west, so will the coming of the Son of Man be. Wherever the corpse is, there the vultures will gather" (Matthew 24:27–28).

 According to Revelation 19:15, who does all of the killing?

_____

Take a few moments to reflect on the image of Christ in blood-soaked robes, riding a white horse, and slaughtering those who rebel against Him. How does this make you feel about Him?

_____

_____

_____

Look back to Revelation 19:14. If the heavenly armies that accompany Christ are unarmed and wear white robes (unstained from the battle), why do you think they are present during the slaughter?

_____

_____

_____

Revelation 19:15 describes the Lord's weapon as a sharp sword from His mouth (see also Revelation 1:16), indicating that it is the spoken word. The author of Hebrews pictured the Word of God as a sword (Hebrews 4:12), as did Paul (Ephesians 6:17), who admonished, "Our struggle is not against flesh and blood, but against the rulers, against the powers, against the world forces of this darkness, against the spiritual forces of wickedness in the heavenly places" (Ephesians 6:12). How absurd for anyone to think that earthly power could offer any advantage in spiritual warfare! The chief weapon of Satan is deception, against which the Lord's truth ultimately prevails.

According to Revelation 19:20, what will happen to the Antichrist and his false prophet?

_____

_____

_____

What will happen to the earthly armies gathered at Har-Megiddo, according to Revelation 19:21?

_____

_____

_____

Do the Antichrist, false prophet, and their armies struggle against their fate? What evidence do you find in these verses?

_____

_____

_____

The mind-set of the earthly armies gathered for battle in the valley is two-dimensional, earthly, and limited to the physical domain. How foolish to point guns and missiles at the all-powerful Creator, who spoke the entire universe into existence and can just as easily destroy it with a mere word! What follows the astonishing appearance of the Lord and the gruesome warning of the angel is

> "not so much a battle as an execution, as the remaining rebels are killed by the Lord Jesus. . . . This Day of the Lord was seen by Isaiah (66:15, 16), Joel (3:12–21), Ezekiel (39:1–4, 17–20), Paul (2 Thess. 1:6ff.; 2:8), and our Lord (Matt. 25:31–46)."[9]

Thus ends the "battle" of Armageddon and the long, terrible reign of evil over the earth, ushering in Christ's triumphant reign.

STARTING YOUR JOURNEY

As we reflect on the implications of Christ's return in power and judgment, three truths will help us understand this future event and its implications for our lives today.

First, *His presence will set the stage in preparation for the final curtain.* Interestingly, John never described exactly how the earth will look when Christ arrives. We know only that those who have chosen to remain His enemies are dead and that His arrival marks the beginning of a completely different earth. John's focus, rightly so, was solely on King Jesus.

In your own words, what does it mean to live in anticipation of Christ's coming as Judge and King?

_____

_____

_____

How does this reality influence your daily behavior? Be specific.

_____

_____

_____

How does this reality influence your long-term plans for the future? Be specific.

_____

_____

_____

Second, *His name will be the final authority*. Ever since the people of Babel (Old Babylon) erected a tower "whose top will reach into heaven" to try to make a name for themselves (Genesis 11:4), humans have sought to replace the name of God with any other authority they could find—self, other gods, money, fame, possessions, and so on. When Christ comes to claim His throne, no other name—no rival authority, no substitute lord—will exist.

If you believe in Jesus Christ as Savior, He is your Lord as well. What person, possession, position, or priority challenges His place on the throne of your heart most often?

_____

_____

_____

How do you typically respond when you realize that you are serving this instead of the Lord?

_____

_____

_____

Third, *His Word will win the final victory*. Christ's return in power will end Satan's reign as "the prince of the power of the air" (Ephesians 2:2) and "the ruler of this world" (John 12:31). With this final battle, Satan will be cast off the throne of the world for all time. As we'll study in the next lesson, he will be allowed one last, desperate attempt to reclaim it, but he will fail. Nothing will unseat the King of kings when He has returned to establish His kingdom.

While the establishment of Christ's physical kingdom on earth is still yet future, He establishes His kingdom in us. In your own words, what does this mean (Jeremiah 31:33–34; John 14:19–23)?

_____

_____

_____

Have you allowed Him to do this in your life? How does your life reflect your decision?

_____

_____

_____

∽✿∾

Jesus came to earth twenty centuries ago and presented Himself as King. When the world, by and large, rejected Him, He returned to heaven after commissioning those who accepted Him to tell others of His eventual return. As word of His arrival spreads, one should be able to easily distinguish between His Majesty's loyal subjects and mere disinterested bystanders. After all, we know this much to be true:

What you *are* determines what you *see*,
and what you *see* determines what you *do*!

LESSON NINE

TURNING THE WORLD RIGHT-SIDE UP

Revelation 20:1–10

THE HEART OF THE MATTER

Following the battle of Armageddon, a great victory for the Lord and His saints, Satan will be bound and sealed away for a thousand years. And Christ will return to establish His kingdom on the earth. At the end of the Millennium (the period of a thousand years), Satan will be released, only to suffer ultimate defeat and be consigned to the abyss with all of his demons forever. Today, we should live in the light of these future events, recognizing that though sin is rampant in our world today, we can rest in the assurance that Satan will one day be defeated and Christ will reign in righteousness for eternity.

In preparation for this lesson, read Revelation 20:1–10.

YOU ARE HERE

Sin spoils everything.

It pollutes skies, cultivates corporate greed, leads to physical and emotional illness, destroys marriages, and inspires wars. It corrupts the legal system, government, economics, and religion. No area within society and culture has escaped sin's sinister hand. Theologian Robert Pyne notes, "A community built on self-interest typically demonstrates the same kinds of sin as an individual. . . . It is difficult for individuals to recognize these collective expressions of sin from within the community, and it is equally difficult to avoid them." [1]

Reflect on some of the ways that sin is currently manifesting itself in government, economics, and religion. Give several specific examples if you can.

_____

_____

_____

_____

How have you personally been affected by sin in these areas of society?

_____

_____

_____

If you were a world leader, how would you try to solve these problems?

_____

_____

_____

DISCOVERING THE WAY

Indeed, the world today is not like it ought to be. Something's wrong. Everybody feels the effects of sin—from the smallest creature to the greatest king.

Read Romans 8:18–25. What does all creation long for, according to this passage?

_____

_____

_____

When will the fulfillment of this prophecy take place?

_____

_____

_____

Will this sinful world ever know true peace and justice? Yes! When Satan is dethroned and King Jesus reigns over this world with all His glorified saints, the world will be renewed. But until then, we must face the reality of a world turned upside-down.

WHAT'S WRONG? WHY AREN'T THINGS AS THEY SHOULD BE?

At the risk of oversimplification, let's offer three objective—though unpopular—reasons why things are not as they should be.

First, *Satan is presently allowed to have his way*. Satan is not a myth or a symbol for evil. He is a real spiritual being who holds sway over many facets of the world—culture, society, politics, economics, and religion (1 John 5:19). For the world to be turned right-side up, Satan must be dethroned.

Second, *Jesus is not yet in authority on the earth*. Christ presently sits at the right hand of the Father (1 Peter 3:22). Christ has received all authority over heaven and earth (Matthew 28:18), but in the present age He has not yet fully taken His authority to reign (Hebrews 2:8; 10:12–13). Because we are still awaiting His enthronement over the earth, our governments are corrupt and sinful. Because Jesus has not yet established His millennial kingdom on earth, the world is still upside-down.

Third, *unrighteous people are in the majority and in authority*. For every good, righteous, and incorruptible leader, there are perhaps dozens of bad, wicked, and debauched ones. They aren't necessarily ignorant, insincere, inexperienced, or lazy people. But they are all sinners, susceptible to the same temptations as every one of us. Proverbs 29:2 states that "When the righteous increase, the people rejoice, / But when a wicked man rules, people groan." To turn the world right-side up and to cause things to be as they were meant to be, righteous rulers need to be in the majority and in authority.

If people cannot bring about the righteous, just, and good society everybody longs for, is there any hope that the world can be turned right-side up?

WHAT'S NEEDED? HOW CAN THINGS BE TURNED RIGHT-SIDE UP? (REVELATION 20:1–6)

The good news is that the book of Revelation promises a Golden Age in which all weapons of warfare will be melted into implements of peace. Prosperity will be shared. Peace will be the banner of all people. The light of justice will illuminate every corner of the world. Theologians call this period of Christ's perfect rule on earth the "millennial kingdom" or the "thousand-year reign."

Read Revelation 20:1–3. Immediately following the return of Christ and the destruction of the Beast, false prophet, and the armies of the earth (Revelation 19:11–21), what will happen to Satan? What will he be unable to do for a thousand years?

_____

_____

_____

Based on this passage, use one word to characterize the extent of Satan's influence over the earth during this thousand-year period.

_____

Imagine a world in which Satan can no longer manipulate leaders, tempt people, gobble up the weak, or corrupt the strong. The complete inability of Satan to exert his wickedness on the earth at that time is made clear by several images in John's vision.

After Satan is bound, the King of kings and His army of saints will come to this earth and take their seats to reign during Satan's thousand-year imprisonment (Revelation 20:4–6). At long last the second reason why things are not as they should be will be resolved. Jesus will take His place of absolute authority over the earth. He will physically reign as King over Israel, and His influence and authority will embrace the entire world.

How does Isaiah 11:1–5 describe the Messiah's reign?

_____

_____

_____

According to Isaiah 11:6–10, what are some of the effects of His rule?

_____

_____

_____

With a perfect, just, and incorruptible King ruling over the world, what current world problems would be eliminated or at least greatly reduced?

_____

_____

_____

Finally, we must note that Christ will not rule alone. All born-again believers who die on earth, having accepted Christ's free gift of salvation, will reign with Him in resurrected, immortal bodies (2 Timothy 2:12; Revelation 5:10). They will sit with Christ on the thrones described in Revelation 20:4. These righteous rulers will not only constitute a moral majority; they will be the only rulers over the earth—unable to be corrupted by money, greed, pride, or power. And if we have a personal relationship with Jesus Christ, we'll be among them!

God's glorified people will enforce the will of Christ and adjudicate disputes between their subjects—those who survive the Tribulation in their mortal bodies (1 Corinthians 6:2). The nation of Israel will be restored to her land through the 144,000 preserved Jews, and Gentile nations will worship and serve the King of kings as inhabitants of the millennial kingdom.

HOW LONG? WILL THIS PEACEFUL KINGDOM LAST FOREVER? (REVELATION 20:2–10)

In one sense, this condition of peace and righteousness *will* last forever. Satan and his false messiah will never regain power. Christ and His saints will never be dethroned. The earth will never again be cursed. Yet in another sense, this specific phase of Christ's rule will come to an end after a thousand years. The numerous descendants of the people who survived the Tribulation period will be tested. Though the original survivors were all believers in Christ, they and their offspring will still have bodies of mortal flesh and will struggle with sin and temptation like we do.

DIGGING DEEPER
The Millennium: Literal or Figurative?

Though a literal reading of Revelation 20:4–6 teaches that a real thousand-year kingdom will be ruled by Christ and the resurrected saints, some theologians throughout church history and today have chosen to interpret this passage figuratively. Some view the resurrection described in Revelation 20:4 as the spiritual resurrection of believers when they are saved and the thousand years as a symbolic number referring to the whole period of the church. Others believe the thousand-year reign refers to Christ and the saints in heaven ruling spiritually for a long period of time.[2] Such interpretations reject the notion that Christ will reign over an earthly kingdom before the final judgment of Revelation 20:7–15.

However, a direct reading of the text argues strongly for a literal kingdom on earth. Jesus's own words in other passages suggest that a literal kingdom will be established upon His return (Matthew 19:28–30; Acts 1:6–8). Also, after the apostles, many prominent church fathers—including Papias, Polycarp, Justin, and Irenaeus—also taught that there would be a literal future thousand-year reign of Christ on earth. This early view of a literal kingdom was slowly replaced by the spiritual interpretation. Saint Augustine, who died early in the fifth century, actually changed his view from a literal kingdom to a spiritual one, and his interpretation has held sway among Catholic and many Protestant theologians ever since.[3]

Read Revelation 20:7–10. How will God test the future generations of humanity at the end of the millennial kingdom?

_____

_____

_____

Even in a perfect world with Christ on the throne, sinful, fallen humans will be deceived by Satan and will rebel against God. What does this tell us about the human heart?

_____

_____

_____

If this is true for people during the Millennium under the perfect rule of Christ, what can we conclude about our own hearts today?

_____

_____

_____

After his thousand-year imprisonment, Satan will be briefly released from the abyss (Revelation 20:7), and he will be allowed to gather "Gog and Magog," a general term for enemies of God spread throughout the earth (Ezekiel 38:2–3; Revelation 20:8). The "war" intended by Satan, however, will never take place. Before a shot is fired, flames from heaven will devour Satan and his vast army of rebels. Then God will finally and permanently consign the devil and all of his cohorts to the lake of fire (Matthew 25:41; Revelation 20:10).

Satan's brief release and humanity's futile rebellion prove two things: *the total incorrigibility of Satan* and *the total depravity of humanity*. As inconceivable as it may seem, not all children born during the Millennium will be believers in Christ. Though Christ's reign will turn the world right-side up, many hearts will remain upside-down.

STARTING YOUR JOURNEY

The events described in Revelation 20:1–10 span a period of a thousand years some time in the future. So, what do these events have to do with us today?

First, we need to *live consistently and realistically while things are upside-down*. As long as this world is not what it ought to be, the best thing we can do is live a life that's right-side up, with a realistic view of the condition of the world—and ourselves. Don't be tricked by people promising lasting peace and prosperity. As long as the devil is on the loose, the world will never be perfect.

Read 1 John 5:19. Though Satan holds sway over the current world system, his power is not absolute. According to the following passages, what things limit Satan's power and activity right now?

Job 2:4–6

_____

Ephesians 6:11–17

_____

James 4:6–7

_____

Based on these passages, what role can you play in resisting Satan's power?

_____

_____

_____

Second, we must *witness faithfully and fervently*. Even a perfect government and just society will not be enough to transform the hearts of sinful humans. Only God can do that. Legislated morality or stricter punishment is not the answer. Positive thinking or psychotherapy won't do the trick. Only Jesus Christ can change the inner life. The coming King died for our sins and rose again so that all who believe can have newness of life in Him.

How does the knowledge that Satan and his cohorts will be completely defeated by God affect your attitude toward sharing your faith with the lost?

_____

_____

_____

Colossians 1:13 says that God "rescued us from the domain of darkness, and transferred us to the kingdom of His beloved Son." As Christians, we have the assurance of eternal life with Christ in the coming kingdom. Today, we have the opportunity to live lives that honor this precious gift. Over the next week, study the following passages, considering the behaviors that would define a kingdom-honoring life, and answer the questions below.

1 Corinthians 6:9–11   Galatians 5:19–25   1 Thessalonians 2:10–12

In the present evil age, as I await Christ's perfect reign, how can I live as a servant of God's kingdom?

_____

_____

_____

According to these passages, is my life right-side up or upside-down?

_____

_____

_____

Sin not only damages our personal lives, but its destructive power permeates all levels of society and culture. Only when Satan is bound and Christ reigns over the earth with His glorified saints will the world be turned right-side up. Yet in that future thousand-year reign, the hearts of humanity will still require the transforming grace of God.

LESSON TEN

THE FINAL EXIT INTERVIEW

Revelation 20:11–15

THE HEART OF THE MATTER
Scenes like the one portrayed in Revelation 20:11–15 keep many people from teaching this book in its entirety. It describes something completely absent from all other passages of Scripture: hopeless finality.

This short paragraph in John's Apocalypse describes the final judgment, in which all the unsaved who have ever lived will be resurrected to stand before God's great white throne to receive their sentencing. The language is clear, direct, pointed, and unembellished. And the facts are set forth without a hint of hope . . . because there is none. No appeal, no debate over guilt or innocence, no final offer of clemency, and no possibility of escape. The purpose of the great white throne judgment is not to decide the fate of the unbeliever. It is a time of sentencing. Our eternal destiny is never decided after death, only before.

In preparation for this lesson, read Revelation 20:11–15.

YOU ARE HERE
The childhood game of hide-and-seek has been around as long as there have been people. In fact, it goes all the way back to the Garden of Eden, where the first people committed the first sin. Adam and Eve lived in perfect harmony with God and with each other in a pristine world—one untainted by self-consciousness, selfishness, or pride. The Bible tells us, "The man and his wife were both naked and were not ashamed" (Genesis 2:25).

Then something terrible occurred. They yielded to temptation and disobeyed God. At once, everything changed.

91

> Then the eyes of both of them were opened, and they knew that they were naked; and they sewed fig leaves together and made themselves loin coverings. They heard the sound of the Lord God walking in the garden in the cool of the day, and the man and his wife hid themselves from the presence of the Lord God among the trees of the garden. (Genesis 3:7–8)

And humankind has been on the run ever since. Why? Paul's letter to the Romans provides the answer. Eugene Peterson's paraphrase renders the apostle's thoughts clearly.

> You know the story of how Adam landed us in the dilemma we're in—first sin, then death, and no one exempt from either sin or death. That sin disturbed relations with God in everything and everyone. (Romans 5:12–13 MSG)

Think of a time when you committed a serious sin against another person. What thoughts and emotions did you experience?

_____

_____

_____

_____

How did you feel about having to interact with this person face-to-face afterward?

_____

_____

_____

How did you eventually resolve the issue?

_____

_____

_____

How do you feel about meeting God, given the fact that you have sinned against Him?

_____

_____

_____

Guilt is a powerful force that propels a person in one of two directions: toward humble repentance or fearful hostility. That's true of our human interactions as well as our relationship with the Lord.

DISCOVERING THE WAY

Revelation 20:11–15 describes a terrible scene — an event no one would want to experience. One fine expositor calls this section "the most serious, sobering, and tragic passage in the entire Bible."[1] The event John saw in his vision will take place after Christ wipes out His enemies at Armageddon, after Satan and his minions are bound for a thousand years while Jesus reigns on the earth, and after evil's last, desperate attempt to regain control of the world. It will take place after Satan, the Antichrist, and his false prophet have been cast into the lake of fire.

NO PLACE TO RUN . . . NO PLACE TO HIDE
(REVELATION 20:11)

This passage opens with the statement, "earth and heaven fled away, and no place was found for them," indicating that all of creation will be removed (Matthew 24:35; 2 Peter 3:10–12; Revelation 21:1). One expositor describes the outcome of this verse in strong terms:

> There is to be an end of the material heavens and earth which we know. It is not that they are purified and rehabilitated, but that the reverse of creation is to take place. They are to be *uncreated*. As they came from nothing at the word of God, they are to be sucked back into nothingness by this same word of God. (emphasis added)[2]

After this, an immeasurable resurrection will take place.

Which people are alive and which remain dead as a result of the events leading up to this resurrection? Read each passage and record who was previously resurrected, raptured, or rescued from death.

1 Thessalonians 4:16 _____

1 Thessalonians 4:17 _____

Revelation 20:4–6 _____

Revelation 20:7 _____

Read the passages below and record which people remain dead or are killed.

Revelation 20:5 _____

Revelation 20:7–9 _____

As your study revealed, the only people raised to life in the second resurrection will be those who died in their sin, apart from Christ—those who rejected His free gift of eternal life. And with no earth and no heaven—no creation at all—they will have nowhere to run and no place to hide. Their self-destructive, deadly game of hide-and-seek will end.

A SET OF BOOKS AND THE BOOK OF LIFE
(REVELATION 20:12)

All unbelievers from all time will stand before a great (symbolizing God's power), white (picturing His purity) throne (representing His authority) (Revelation 20:11). And they will be judged.

As a part of the proceedings, a set of books will be opened in addition to the Book of Life (Revelation 20:12). What information do you think this set of books contains?

_____

_____

_____

What information does the Book of Life contain (see Revelation 20:15)?

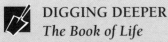

DIGGING DEEPER
The Book of Life

The "Book of Life" is a New Testament concept with deep roots in the Old Testament (Exodus 32:32–33; Daniel 12:1–2; Malachi 3:16). Believers during Old Testament times were saved by grace, through faith, as they honored the Old Covenant. When Jesus initiated the New Covenant, He told His disciples to "rejoice that your names are recorded in heaven" (Luke 10:20). Paul encouraged believers with a reminder that their names were written in the Book of Life alongside other faithful servants of Jesus (Philippians 4:3), and the author of Hebrews declared that the church comprised those "who are enrolled in heaven" (Hebrews 12:23).

In order for a person's name to be recorded in the Book of Life, he or she must reject the notion that his or her own righteousness will suffice. As the apostle Paul wrote, "[A person] is not justified by the works of the Law but through faith in Christ Jesus, even we have believed in Christ Jesus, so that we may be justified by faith in Christ and not by the works of the Law; since by the works of the Law no flesh will be justified" (Galatians 2:16). Believers—whose names are written in the Book of Life—are never judged by their deeds and will not be present at the great white throne judgment.

Revelation 20:12 tells us that another set of books records the good and bad deeds of every person.

At the end of all time, each person will be judged by the contents of either the Book of Life or the set of books recording his or her deeds. Anyone has the option to reject the Book of Life and have his or her life judged by the deeds recorded in the other books. If he or she has only good deeds recorded there, *with no sins whatsoever*, that person will be worthy of heaven. However, God's standard is complete moral perfection. If He finds just one sin recorded there, no matter

Continued on next page

Continued from previous page

how small, the sentence will be an eternity of suffering in the lake of fire. No one except the Son of God has ever lived without sinning (2 Corinthians 5:21). And because we are all humans with depraved natures, living in a fallen world, no one ever will (Romans 3:23).

Fortunately, we have the opportunity *today* to choose which record will be used at the end of time. However, when we die, it will be too late. To learn more about how you can have your name permanently inscribed in the Book of Life, turn to the section at the end of this Bible Companion titled, "How to Begin a Relationship with God."

THE FINAL EXIT INTERVIEW (REVELATION 20:12–15)

In Revelation 20:12–13, the phrase "the great and the small," along with the later assertions that the sea, death, and Hades "gave up the dead," indicates that all people through all time who rejected God's grace—all unbelievers—will be made to stand before Him and receive judgment. As you read Revelation 20:12–15 once more, note the repetition of the phrase "according to their deeds." The purpose of this appearance before the Creator is to allow the charges to be read to each and every unbeliever before sentencing. As one expositor put it,

> The accused, all the unsaved who have ever lived, will be resurrected to experience a trial like no other that has ever been. There will be no debate over their guilt or innocence. There will be a prosecutor, but no defender; an accuser but no advocate. There will be an indictment, but no defense mounted by the accused; the convicting evidence will be presented with no rebuttal or cross-examination. There will be an utterly unsympathetic Judge and no jury, and there will be no appeal of the sentence He pronounces. The guilty will be punished eternally with no possibility of parole in a prison from which there is no escape.[3]

John calls this judgment "the second death." And no one who attends the great white throne judgment will escape it.

What Happens to a Person After Death?

"And inasmuch as it is appointed for men to die once and after this comes judgment." (Hebrews 9:27)

	At Death	Bodily Resurrection	Judgment	Eternal Destination
Christian	Christ's Presence The Grave	Resurrection at the Rapture	Judgment Seat of Christ in Heaven for Rewards	Heaven
Old Testament Believer	Paradise/ Abraham's Bosom The Grave	Resurrection at Christ's Second Coming	Judgment on Earth for Rewards	Heaven
Tribulation Believer	Christ's Presence The Grave	Resurrection at Christ's Second Coming	Judgment on Earth for Rewards	Heaven
Unbeliever	Sheol/Hades Torment The Grave	Resurrection at the End of the Millennium	Judgment at the Great White Throne for Sins	Hell/ Gehenna/ Lake of Fire

STARTING YOUR JOURNEY

In your study of John's vision of the future in Revelation 20:11–15, you may have noticed that no one's eternal destiny was debated. John's language is clear and blunt, leaving little room for misunderstanding. Those in the first resurrection will reign with Christ (Revelation 20:6), while those in the second resurrection will suffer eternal punishment in hell. Deciding which resurrection we will join has been left to us—a choice to be made only in this life. When all people stand before God—the believers to receive rewards, the unbelievers at the great white throne to receive punishment—He will merely mete out the consequences of the choice we made while on earth.

How do we receive eternal life? One word—*Christ.*

And when should we make that choice? Again, one word—*now.*

Has the gospel been clearly presented to you in terms you can understand? (If not, we invite you to contact Insight for Living Pastoral Ministries. See "We Are Here for You" at the back of this Bible Companion for contact information.) If so, how did you respond?

_____

_____

_____

If you have not already done so, what is keeping you from turning to Christ for salvation from the penalty of sin—eternity in the lake of fire?

_____

_____

_____

If you have accepted Christ's gift of salvation, perhaps now would be a good time to pray for someone you know who has not yet chosen to join the first resurrection. What, as far as you know, keeps him or her running and hiding from God? Make this issue the focus of your prayer.

_____

_____

_____

John's purpose in describing the great white throne judgment is clear. With chilling simplicity and candor, he reveals the eternal consequences of rejecting God's free gift of salvation by grace through faith in Jesus Christ. This decision must not be postponed, for anyone's life could end before sunrise tomorrow. At the moment of his or her death, the decision a person makes will be sealed forever.

Choose wisely.

LESSON ELEVEN

HEAVEN AT LAST

Revelation 21:1–8

THE HEART OF THE MATTER

When God created the world, He intended it to be ideally suited for humankind, whom He created to enjoy an intimate relationship with Him forever. While sin interrupted the Lord's purpose for us and made the world a difficult place to live, evil will not have the last word. After the final judgment at the great white throne, God will create a new universe to replace the one He "uncreated" in Revelation 20:11. This "new heaven and new earth" (Revelation 21:1) is the future hope of all who know and love the Lord Jesus Christ. It will be very different from the sin-twisted, broken-down universe we see today. All the things that cause us grief and sorrow will be no more . . . it will be filled with what we were created to enjoy: the presence of God. And while we eagerly anticipate this future existence, we can enjoy God's presence here and now—but only if we heed God's call to join Him where He is.

In preparation for this lesson, read Revelation 21:1–8.

YOU ARE HERE

The *Westminster Shorter Catechism* begins with a very intriguing question: "What is the chief end of man?" [1] The word "end" refers to both our primary purpose and our ultimate destiny. When believers are asked the question, "If you were to die today, where would you go?" most will answer with assurance, "Heaven!" However, when asked, "What is your purpose? Why did God create you?" very few can answer with any confidence.

What do you believe to be your primary purpose in life? Why were you created?

_____

_____

_____

To what degree do you feel you live out this purpose in your life? What specific struggles seem to hinder you?

_____

_____

_____

How do you think your life would be different if you actually did what you were created to do?

_____

_____

_____

DISCOVERING THE WAY

The *Westminster Shorter Catechism* proposes the following answer to its first question: "Man's chief end is to glorify God, and to enjoy him forever."[2] "In the beginning God created the heavens and the earth" (Genesis 1:1), and He fashioned it perfectly to suit our needs. He communed with the first humans as they lived according to their design, giving glory to God and enjoying Him. But as we know from Genesis 3:1–24, the first humans disobeyed God, subjecting the whole world to the awful effects of sin. Even as the people rebelled against God, so the earth rebelled against the people, and the universe has been a continual source of grief and sorrow ever since.

Enter Revelation. Having witnessed the "uncreation" of the original heaven and earth (Revelation 20:11), we glimpse in Revelation 21 the brand-new, uncorrupted home where God intends for us to spend eternity.

A DESCRIPTION OF OUR HEAVENLY HOME

Revelation 21:1–8 serves as a short preview for what John will describe in greater detail in 21:9–22:5. In those verses, he will do his best to describe the new universe using familiar images and symbols to represent a reality that is far beyond what we can imagine. But his purpose in verses 1–8 is merely to assure us that the new heaven and earth will be very different from what we experience today.

NEW AND IMPROVED! (REVELATION 21:1–2)

The "new heaven and a new earth" will not be new in merely a chronological sense, but also in a qualitative sense. John used the Greek word *kainos* to convey the concept of "new." It means, "what is new in nature, different from the usual, impressive, better than the old, superior in value or attraction."[3] After the first heaven and earth has "fled away" (Revelation 20:11), along with all the associated contaminations of sin, God will speak a new universe, a *kainos* universe, into existence (Revelation 21:1). This new earth will contain no sea, and it will be ruled from a new capital city.

DOORWAY TO HISTORY
No More Sea

Today we view the sea as necessary "to cleanse the earth and make life possible. . . . The antiseptic salinity of the sea absorbs, scrubs, and breaks down . . . pollutants and wastes. The sun heats the sea, causing only pure, clean water vapor to float up into the sky, forming clouds which bring refreshing rain back to the land—a continuous cycle of cleansing and renewal."[4]

But to ancient people, the sea was a mysterious, dangerous place, characterized by chaos and possessing the power to kill without warning. No fate could have been worse than to be swallowed by the sea and have one's remains eaten by fish. "Both Greeks and Romans . . . recoiled with great horror at the thought of death by drowning or even burial at sea."[5] Furthermore, biblical cosmology

Continued on next page

Continued from previous page

considered the heavens, the earth (dry land), and the sea to be the fundamental components of the universe (see Psalm 135:6; Haggai 2:6; Acts 4:24; Revelation 5:13).[6] So, failing to mention the sea when describing the universe would have left a number of questions unanswered.

For John, the sea acted as a symbol, "a principle of disorder, violence, or unrest that marks the old creation (cf. Isa. 57:20; Ps. 107:25–28; Ezek. 28:8)."[7] His usage of the sea elsewhere in Revelation designates it as the origin of cosmic evil (Revelation 12:12; 13:1; 15:2) or the unbelieving nations who persecute God's people (Revelation 12:12; 13:1). He also uses it symbolically to refer to the old creation (Revelation 5:13; 7:1–3; 8:8–9; 10:2, 5–6, 8; 14:7).[8]

In describing the new creation, John made a specific point of mentioning that "there is no longer any sea" (Revelation 21:1), illustrating that the very cosmology of the universe would be completely different. Ancient people would have been dismayed and a little perplexed to hear that a perfect universe included a sea. And according to modern science, a perfect world has no need for one.

HOW THEN WE SHALL LIVE (REVELATION 21:3–6)

The new creation will be very different from our existing world in several other respects. The sea is but the first of the earthly components that will not exist in the newly created universe.

What four negative aspects of the old creation will be missing from the new creation, according to Revelation 21:4?

_____

_____

_____

_____

What does Revelation 22:3 say will end that began in Genesis 3:14–19?

_____

What significant feature of the old universe will not exist in the new (Revelation 21:25; 22:5)?

_____

Read Revelation 21:3, 23–24 and 22:5. Why will night cease to exist?

_____

_____

Ever since the first people introduced sin into the world, we have struggled to fulfill our purpose against a cursed creation. In the new creation, at last we will be rid of all encumbrances that keep us from glorifying God and enjoying Him forever. Moreover, all that makes this world painful or sorrowful will be replaced by the shining presence of God—just as light displaces darkness. He will live with His believers, and in His presence *life is good*!

Read Revelation 21:3–7. List several words or phrases to describe the quality of life that believers will enjoy with God.

_____

_____

_____

How is this different from the way that believers live in relation to Him now?

_____

_____

_____

In Revelation 21:6, God utters the phrase, "It is done. . . . I will give to the one who thirsts from the spring of the water of life without cost." This verse indicates that the people who inhabit the new creation will indeed thirst, though not for water in the literal sense (John 4:10, 13–14). The future inhabitants of heaven will have a need—just as people do now—to fulfill their created purpose: "to glorify God and to enjoy Him forever." And they will never thirst, because what they need they will have in abundance.

WHO WILL BE THERE (REVELATION 21:7–8)

At this point in the future, believers and nonbelievers will live eternally, though in very different places. One of John's primary purposes for writing was to convince those who have not placed their faith in Christ to do so. At several junctions in the text, he reminded the reader of God's offer of salvation and of the certain consequences that follow a failure to respond.

Who, according to Revelation 21:7, will "inherit these things"?

_____

_____

In the same verse, to what does the phrase "these things" refer?

_____

_____

Who qualifies to be called one "who overcomes"? (For help, read 1 John 5:4–5.)

_____

_____

According to Revelation 21:8, who will not partake in the new creation?

_____

_____

What is to be their fate?

_____

_____

_____

Like Paul did on other occasions, John distinguishes those who do not believe from those who do believe by listing several typical sins of which they are guilty (1 Corinthians 6:9–10; Galatians 5:19–21). While *all* people are guilty of these sins—and more—only those who do not believe are identified by them. Because the sins of those who believe in Christ have been removed, Christians are identified by their faith.

STARTING YOUR JOURNEY

As we turn from study to application, pause to consider three simple statements.

First, *any place God plans to be, you want to be there.*

At the beginning of this lesson, you were asked to state what you believe to be your purpose in life—the reason you were created. Our study of this passage may have caused you to reconsider or modify your response. Hopefully, you will have found some measure of relief in knowing that *how* you glorify God and enjoy Him is not nearly as important as how *much* or how *often.* In truth, the Lord merely invites us to draw close to Him, leaving the decisions on *how* largely with us. Endless opportunities to commune with God are all around us.

To glorify God means "to make glorious by bestowing honor, praise, or admiration." [9] For each of the areas below, indicate one specific way you can glorify God and enjoy Him.

Worship: _____

Charity: _____

Community: _____

Vocation: _____

Study: _____

Relaxation: _____

Labor: _____

What keeps you from living out your purpose in these ways?

_____

_____

_____

Second, *anything God removes, you don't need.*

While the Lord allows us the freedom to engage Him in a variety of ways, ultimately He directs the process. Very often that involves removing distractions. In the new creation, we will not have an old sin nature and its petty lusts to contend with. But until then, He will have to restrict us from elevating anything above Him, which may mean removing legitimate sources of happiness to which we have given illegitimate love or devotion.

In the past, what has the Lord removed from your life that was a distraction from fellowship with Him? Briefly describe it below.

_____

_____

_____

The Lord delights for us to enjoy His blessings, but never at the risk of our intimacy with Him. What object(s) of love in your life might threaten your relationship with God? What will you do about it?

_____

_____

_____

Third, *any time God makes an offer, you're wise to accept it.*

Because the Lord made you, He knows better than anyone—even you—what will best serve your interests. He repeatedly presents us with opportunities and invites us to partake in what will make us happy and fulfilled, if only we will heed His direction.

Take a few moments in silence to reflect on your relationship with God. What offer has the Lord made that will allow you to glorify and enjoy Him more?

_____

_____

_____

What have you done in response? What will you do next?

_____

_____

_____

❧

Each of us was created with a thirst to fulfill our purpose. Many wander through life trying to discover the right vocation, the right relationship, the right possessions, the right knowledge—the list of substitutes for a relationship with the Lord is endless—all in an effort to discover personal meaning, to feel significant, or to find satisfaction. The living water we seek is free, abundant, and can be found only in our Creator. And as we seek to glorify God, we will discover something marvelous occurring within: we will enjoy Him!

Lesson Twelve

Open House at the Celestial City

Revelation 21:9–22

 THE HEART OF THE MATTER

John's detailed description of the New Jerusalem answers our most common questions regarding paradise by using unexpected images. As we take in the incredible scenes, it might help to think of this journey as a guided tour through a gallery of beautiful, priceless works of art displayed for all to savor. But keep in mind that, in truth, this is no gallery, but an inspired, prophetic unveiling of the place where we will spend eternity. Though some things will remain a mystery, this glimpse of our future should encourage us to live in joyful anticipation of that which awaits us.

In preparation for this lesson, read Revelation 21:9–22.

 YOU ARE HERE

All of us have driven or walked past a house—what we might call a mansion—that catches our attention and makes our imaginations run wild. Who lives there? What's it like inside? When was it built? We may picture ornate rooms filled with antique furniture, walls draped with tapestries, or works of art lining the hallways. But unless we see a sign that reads "Open House," most of us will never satisfy our curiosity or feed our imaginations with reality.

Heaven is the same way. For so many, the idea of our eternal home is just that: *an idea*. And unless we receive an invitation to experience an open house at the Celestial City, none of us can begin to fathom its wonders.

If somebody were to ask you what heaven will be like, how would you respond? Form your answer as if you were responding to a person who has no background in the Bible.

_____

_____

_____

_____

_____

_____

If you could ask Jesus three questions about your eternal home, what would they be?

1. _____

2. _____

3. _____

DISCOVERING THE WAY

As we accept our invitation to God's open house at the Celestial City, we will discover some important truths. First, our limited expectations about what heaven is like may not reflect the amazing reality. In many ways, heaven will exceed the limits of our imaginations. Second, our questions about heaven may be misguided ones. God's purpose and plan for our eternal home far surpasses our limited, temporal curiosities.

THE PREDICTION OF A PREPARED PLACE (JOHN 14:1–3)

In one of His precious last moments with His disciples, Jesus encouraged them with a promise of things to come:

> "Do not let your heart be troubled; believe in God, believe also in Me. In My Father's house are many dwelling places; if it were not so, I would have told you; for I go to prepare a place for you. If I go and

prepare a place for you, I will come again and receive you to Myself, that where I am, there you may be also." (John 14:1–3)

The disciples heard the promise of a place, and they knew the way: through Christ (John 14:6). But what would it be like? For that answer, John would have to wait more than sixty years.

THE DESCRIPTION OF OUR HEAVENLY HOME (REVELATION 21:9–22)

In the previous lesson, our lens caught an establishing shot of the New Jerusalem—a rare and precious glimpse of heaven from afar. In this lesson we will zoom in for a close-up shot. As we drop from an aerial perspective into the midst of the Celestial City, we will soar across the glimmering cityscape, examine the details of its structure, and bask in its glory. In particular, we will explore the origin, appearance, exterior, dimensions, materials, and distinctive of God's eternal city.

First, let's look at the *origin of the Celestial City* (Revelation 21:9–10). As God's final judgment upon unrepentant sinners fades into the distance, one of the seven angels who had poured out the bowls of wrath takes center stage to serve as John's escort on his tour of the New Jerusalem.

Read Hebrews 11:10; 12:22; and Revelation 21:1–2. Why is it important that the origin of the New Jerusalem is in God and not in man? What does this imply about the origin of your own salvation? Read Ephesians 2:8–10 and incorporate it into your answer.

_____

_____

_____

Second, John focused on the *appearance of the Celestial City* (Revelation 21:11). In his inspired description of the New Jerusalem, John used two words to convey its stunning appearance: "glory" and "brilliance." Both of these emphasize that God is not only the originator of the city (Revelation 21:9–10), but He is also the one who illuminates and sustains it with His divine power and presence.

GETTING TO THE ROOT

The Greek words translated as "glory" and "brilliance" in Revelation 21:11 are *doxa* and *phōstēr*. The "glory of God," also mentioned in Revelation 15:8 and 21:23, most likely refers to the glowing presence of God (called "the Shekinah" by Jewish teachers) both among His people and within the tabernacle and temple as described in the Old Testament (Exodus 40:34–35; Ezekiel 43:5).[1] When John compares this brilliant glory of God to a "jasper" stone (the Greek word *iaspis*), he probably does not mean the modern-day stone called "jasper," but rather an unblemished diamond. One commentator notes: "Heaven's capital city is thus pictured as a huge, flawless diamond, refracting the brilliant, blazing glory of God throughout the new heaven and the new earth."[2] Nothing on earth begins to compare to what God has prepared for us, and words fail to capture the breathtaking intensity of His glory.

Next, our guide gives us a survey of the *exterior of the Celestial City* (Revelation 21:12–14).

Based on John's description in Revelation 21:12–14, sketch the city's walls, gates, and foundations. Make it as simple or detailed as you like.

In light of Paul's words in Ephesians 2:11–22, what do the inscriptions on the foundations and gates of the New Jerusalem tell us about the inhabitants?

_____

_____

_____

Fourth, let's consider the *dimensions of the Celestial City* (Revelation 21:15–17). The size of the city is staggering—nearly 1,500 miles along one wall. When we realize that this is the capital city of God's new creation and that its origin is from God Himself, we should not be surprised at its incredible size. It will be the eternal dwelling place of countless saints from all of human history.

Fifth, John describes the *materials of the Celestial City* (Revelation 21:18–21). Moving from the structure and size, our lens zooms in closer to the actual texture and color of the walls, gates, and foundations, and we observe several important characteristics. First, the foundations of the city are adorned with a wide variety of jewels (Revelation 21:19–20). Such materials may symbolize the diversity of people that will dwell within the city's walls. Second, the city itself is "crystal clear" and the massive wall surrounding it is transparent (21:11, 18). The city and its inhabitants have nothing to hide and no need for privacy. Instead, God's glory shines from within. Third, each gate leading into the city is created from one giant pearl.

Finally, let's ponder the *distinctive of the Celestial City* (Revelation 21:22). If one were to ask you, "What was the central feature of the old city of Jerusalem?" you would probably answer, "The temple." So, as John's wide-angle view of the New Jerusalem narrows toward its center, we would expect to see the eternal edition of this primary place of worship.

According to Revelation 21:22, what is the temple of the New Jerusalem?

_____

_____

_____

What do the following passages emphasize about worship after Christ's first coming? Summarize what each tells us about how and where we are to worship today.

John 4:20–24

_____

_____

_____

Romans 12:1–2

_____

_____

_____

1 Corinthians 3:10–17 (Note that "you" in verse 16 is plural, "you all.")

_____

_____

_____

In the present age of the church, God redirects the location of worship from a physical temple in Jerusalem to the spiritual "temple" of the universal church—the body of believers. In the future New Jerusalem, in which all the redeemed of every age will dwell, the center of worship will be the Father and the Son, and the saints will worship forever in the power of the Holy Spirit.

STARTING YOUR JOURNEY

At the beginning of this lesson, you jotted down your own description of your eternal home as well as some questions you have about the Celestial City. Chances are your description contained some inaccuracies—or at least emphasized things that John's description in Revelation 21 does not. Also, you probably asked questions that remain unanswered even after John's detailed description of the origin, appearance, exterior, dimensions, materials, and distinctive. Most of our questions will not be fully answered until we see this city for ourselves. John's open-house tour whets our appetite for more but leaves much more to be explored. And though we could dig deeper into the profound significance of many aspects of John's description, let's focus on two observations about the Celestial City that we can relate to our present lives.

First, we see that *the city and wall will be of transparent gold to let the glory of God shine through*. In the present age, people build walls to maintain privacy and security. These can be physical barriers to keep our neighbors from watching our every move, but they can also be mental, emotional, or spiritual walls that protect us from harm, hide our shame, or keep people at a distance. This kind of secrecy and security will be completely unnecessary in the Celestial City. And to a certain degree, Christians today can reflect the grace and glory of God, not by hiding in the "inner sanctuary" of life but by being transparent to others.

Think about one person who has touched your life deeply. Has this person been transparent with you regarding his or her struggles, triumphs, and spiritual walk? How have you seen the grace and glory of God reflected in his or her life? How has this affected you?

_____

_____

_____

_____

Do you struggle with revealing your thoughts, emotions, and even actions to others? Why, or why not? If so, what do you fear most?

_____

_____

_____

If you knew that you could encourage someone else by living a more transparent life, would you be willing to try? Who might benefit if you were to share your struggles as a means of encouragement?

_____

_____

_____

The second thing we notice about the Celestial City that parallels a truth in the Christian life is that *the gates will be constructed of massive pearls.* John Phillips writes:

> All other precious gems are metals or stones, but a pearl is a gem formed within the oyster—the only one formed by living flesh. The humble oyster receives an irritation or wound, and around the offending article that has penetrated and hurt it, the oyster builds a pearl. The pearl, we might say, is the answer of the oyster to that which injured it.[3]

When we read of this eternal symbol of suffering crowned with glory, it reminds us that Christ's suffering had an eternal purpose and opened heaven for us (John 10:9; 14:6). It also assures us that our own suffering for the sake of Christ has a purpose and can be used by Him to reflect His glory in our lives.

What positive results of suffering are revealed in the following passages?

Romans 5:3–5

_____

_____

_____

Philippians 3:8–11

_____

_____

_____

James 1:2–4

_____

_____

_____

Have you personally experienced an occasion when God turned your sorrow into joy or your pain into pearls? Briefly describe the situation, and then take a few moments to pray, thanking Him for leading you through the trial and for teaching you along the way.

_____

_____

_____

_____

_____

_____

We all have expectations about heaven. Some of them are unrealistic. Others reflect our own earthly values and desires. Some are just plain incorrect. The few glimpses of our eternal home given to us in Scripture, however, hint at something far greater and more glorious than we can imagine. As we look forward to our heavenly home, we can also live our lives today with a heavenly perspective.

LESSON THIRTEEN

HEAVEN'S MAGNIFICENT NEGATIVES

Revelation 21:21–22:5

 THE HEART OF THE MATTER
Life on planet Earth has a number of perils, not the least of which is an earthbound perspective that threatens to obscure our vision of heaven. Space and time define the boundaries of our universe, while the curse of sin dictates how it functions. These concepts fail to apply in heaven. Furthermore, the things we value most in this existence will have little or no meaning then. The new creation—heaven—will be so dramatically different from anything we can possibly imagine that words literally fail to express it.

To describe this new creation to people who are bound by space, time, and the Curse, in the book of Revelation the Lord employs a series of negative statements to reveal what will *not* be there, giving familiar images a surprising new twist. This meaningful glimpse into something far beyond our comprehension strengthens our hope and encourages us to endure the pain of this life with courage.

In preparation for this lesson, read Revelation 21:21–22:5.

 YOU ARE HERE
The world in which we live operates by a set of rules that we often regard as unchangeable truth. In fact, we're so sure of their immutable nature that we set them down in pithy maxims and pass them on to the next generation. For instance:

"You get what you pay for."

"There's no such thing as a free lunch."

"You only live once."

"Let the buyer beware."

"If something can go wrong, it will."

"To err is human . . ."

"All good things must come to an end."

Because of sin, the world operates by principles that are very contrary to those that were originally established by God "in the beginning" (Genesis 1:1). Now, after the Fall, we can rightfully say, "There's something wrong with everything."

What is your greatest frustration or sorrow in life? How have you chosen to deal with it?

_____

_____

_____

_____

What is your greatest fear, and how does it influence how you live?

_____

_____

_____

_____

What in this life gives you (or would give you) the greatest delight?

_____

_____

_____

Do these factors keep you from fulfilling your purpose? In what ways?

_____

_____

_____

_____

DISCOVERING THE WAY

Before the Fall and the Curse, the universe operated by a different set of rules—the Lord's rules. As we discovered in our study of Revelation 20, evil will be destroyed forever; however, the new creation will not merely reflect the earth in its pre-Fall condition. It will be qualitatively different from the old, even before the first creation was twisted by sin.

Heaven will be so foreign to earthly categories that it defies description. It will involve realities so removed from our experience that we have no vocabulary to represent the features of that unimaginable world. The most effective way the Lord can overcome our limitations is to explain what will *not* be present.

A WORLD WITHOUT WANT (REVELATION 21:21)

Revelation 21:18–21 describes the materials used to construct the New Jerusalem. All of them would have been impressive to the first-century reader, but the idea of streets paved with gold would have been particularly surprising. The marble-paved streets of Ephesus were an unusual extravagance, designating it as one of the most opulent cities in the Roman Empire. Nevertheless, most of the material came from dismantled buildings. The builders used recycled marble, and it was still considered a remarkable display.

The opulence of the New Jerusalem will far exceed that of Ephesus or any other city. It will be paved with gold so pure it will be transparent like glass. Whether or not this is a strictly literal feature of the new creation, the point is the same. Heaven considers gold—a costly, precious commodity in the old creation—no more valuable than asphalt or concrete!

No one is poor in a place that paves its streets with gold. The new creation will be a world without want.

Imagine what your life would be like if you had need of nothing—if you didn't have to work for a paycheck, never had any debts to pay, and had an abundance of not only food and clothing but also luxuries. And what if you were always spiritually and relationally satisfied? If all of these things were provided for you, how would your priorities change? What would you do with all of your extra time?

_____

_____

_____

_____

WORSHIP WITHOUT A BUILDING (REVELATION 21:22)

We tend to associate impressive structures with religious activity, such as the massive, ornate buildings of the Vatican or the Al-Aqsa Mosque in Jerusalem with its enormous golden dome. Even smaller structures such as our own churches represent to us sacred places where we learn about and worship God. But the New Jerusalem will have no need for a special building set aside for worship.

A CITY WITHOUT DARKNESS (REVELATION 21:23–24; 22:5)

Revelation 21:23–24 and 22:5 describe the new creation's most unusual feature. On the fourth day of the first Creation, the Lord created lights to illumine the earth and to mark time (Genesis 1:14–19). The new creation will not need sources of light because God will illumine heaven with His glory. This detail points to a very profound truth about how different the New Jerusalem will be from our present experience.

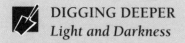

DIGGING DEEPER
Light and Darkness

Throughout the Bible, the concepts of light and darkness are used to describe the two opposing cosmic realms:

truth   vs.   error (John 3:21; 1 John 1:5–8)

God's created order   vs.   sin's corruption (John 1:1–5)

spirit   vs.   flesh (Romans 13:12–14)

God's Kingdom   vs.   the Satan-governed world (Colossians 1:13–14)

Moses told us in Genesis 1 that after God created the heavens and the earth, He created light. This is both literal and symbolic. In response to the many pagan creation myths that influenced the Hebrews leaving Egypt, Moses wanted God's people to know that the Lord created the universe and infused it with truth, as He is the author of truth.

After the introduction of sin, the world no longer operated the way God originally designed it. Twisted by the Fall and obedient to Satan, it began to function according to a competing system, which poets and other writers called "darkness" (Psalm 107:10–11; Proverbs 2:13; 4:19; Isaiah 5:20; 9:2; 42:6–7; Matthew 6:22–23; Luke 1:78–79; John 1:5; Romans 2:17–21; Colossians 1:13–14). Then, light invaded the darkness in the person of Jesus Christ (John 1:1–5; 8:12; 12:35–36, 46). According to John, the truth Christ lived, taught, and placed within believers is also the light in which He calls us to walk (1 John 1:5–7).

When John said that night will no longer exist in the newly created universe, he was speaking both literally and symbolically. In the new creation, error, sin's corruption, "the flesh" (our old, worldly, selfish way of thinking and living), and the evil administration of the world will be replaced—as light displaces darkness—by the holy, shining presence of God.

SECURITY WITHOUT LOCKS (REVELATION 21:25–26)

The sole purpose for an ancient city's wall was security. And no part of the wall could be more important than its gates. In the New Jerusalem, the gates will never close (Revelation 21:25) because there is no evil to shut out.

If you were to move into a community in which everyone left their doors and windows unlocked and always left their car key in the ignition, how would you explain their behavior?

_____

_____

_____

With your previous answer in mind, what do the open gates of the new creation signify?

_____

_____

LIFE WITHOUT THE CURSE (REVELATION 21:27; 22:3)

In the beginning, God created the earth to be perfectly suited for human life: security without locks, food without famine, work without toil, no weeds, no enmity, no self-consciousness nor fear. But all of that changed when the first people introduced sin into the world (Genesis 3:14–19). According to Revelation 21:27 and 22:3, heaven will be untouched by the Curse.

Read Genesis 3:15–19. What cursed aspects of earthly life will be missing in the new creation?

Genesis 3:15 __Hostility between the serpent (evil) and people_____

Genesis 3:16a _____

Genesis 3:16b _____

Genesis 3:17 _____

Genesis 3:18 _____

Genesis 3:19 _____

CONTENTMENT WITHOUT END (REVELATION 22:5)

One aspect of existence in this present world can be expressed in the maxim, "All good things must come to an end." Picnics, roller coaster rides, vacations, careers, and most relationships all end. Furthermore, the unrelenting progress of time carries us toward the most reprehensible and tragic result of sin: death.

Read Revelation 22:2. What feature from the Garden of Eden will be made available to people again in the new creation? (See Genesis 3:22–24.)

_____

_____

_____

Revelation 22:1 mentions a "river of the water of life." What do you think this represents? (See John 4:7, 13–14.)

_____

_____

_____

STARTING YOUR JOURNEY

Jim Elliot, a missionary among the Quichua Indians of Ecuador, pondered the return of Christ and the prospect of heaven. In his private writings, he offered the following prayer:

O Jesus, Master and Center and End of all, how long before that Glory is Thine which has so long waited Thee? Now there is no thought of Thee among men; then there shall be thought for nothing else. Now other men are praised; then none shall care for any other's merits. Hasten, hasten, Glory of Heaven, take Thy crown, subdue Thy Kingdom, enthrall Thy creatures.[1]

The close, personal friendship Jim Elliot cultivated with his Lord animated his zeal for ministry and energized his enthusiasm for life in general. And a significant part of that relationship was his eternal perspective. How well have you cultivated this aspect of your spiritual life? *It's difficult to ignore eternity.*

Based on your study of Revelation 21:21–22:5, describe how you imagine life in the new creation, especially as it relates to your greatest frustration, sorrow, or fear.

_____

_____

_____

_____

Thinking about your greatest delight on earth, how will it be different in heaven?

_____

_____

_____

_____

How does knowledge of this future affect your ability to endure hardship?

_____

_____

_____

If you were to meditate regularly on the glories of heaven and the coming opportunity to enjoy the Lord forever, what effect do you think it would have on your spiritual life?

_____

_____

_____

_____

As an experiment over the next week, set aside a regular time each day to read Revelation 21:1–22:5 and journal what you think your life will be like in the new creation. Be specific. Think creatively. Allow your imagination to run.

At the end of the week, reflect on the influence the exercise had on your attitude, your decisions, your ability to cope with stress, and your interactions with others.

In the new creation, evil, sorrow, suffering, sin, and selfishness will not exist. Death will be a distant memory of another existence. All good things will *never* come to an end as His people give glory to God and enjoy Him forever.

In January of 1951, Jim Elliot began the final stretch of his preparation for ministry among the Quichua Indians of Ecuador. In his carefully kept journal, he contemplated the future he would enjoy.

> Oh, the fullness, pleasure, sheer excitement of knowing God on earth. I care not if I never raise my voice again for Him, if only I may love Him, please Him. Mayhap, in mercy, He shall give me a host of children that I may lead through the vast star fields to explore His delicacies whose fingers' ends set them to burning. But if not, if only I may see Him, smell His garments, and smile into my Lover's eyes, ah, then, not stars, nor children, shall matter—only Himself.[2]

On January 8, 1956, Jim and four other missionaries entered Glory after giving their earthly lives to share the good news of Jesus Christ with the Waorani Indians.

LESSON FOURTEEN

COMPELLING WORDS FOR
A CONFUSED CULTURE

Revelation 22:6–16

THE HEART OF THE MATTER

Paul warned his young protégé, Timothy, that a primary characteristic of the latter days will be the widespread rejection of truth (1 Timothy 4:1–2; 2 Timothy 4:3–4). John's Apocalypse provides exactly what the coming end-times generation—and every generation—needs: objective, certified, reliable truth. When armed with truth, people can face with greater security, faith, and courage the "deceitful spirits," "doctrines of demons," and "hypocrisy of liars" that define the latter days.

In preparation for this lesson, read Revelation 22:6–16.

YOU ARE HERE

The twentieth century saw the rise of a generation that not only rejected much of what their elders held to be true, but even began to doubt the existence of truth as a concept. The tragic result has been a philosophical system that many sociologists call "relativism" or "postmodernism." It is the belief that truth should be defined as merely the commonly held beliefs of a particular culture or society and may or may not be valid for another culture or society. Through the media, academia, and other aspects of culture, this idea continues to shape the thinking of many, if not most, people living in the twenty-first century, whether they realize it or not. And younger generations are left to grope their way aimlessly through a relativistic fog, feeling insecure, fearful, and weak.

What specific examples of moral relativism or indefinite truth do you see in today's world?

_____

_____

_____

What effect do you think relativism has on young people as they mature?

_____

_____

If someone doubts the existence of objective truth, what effect will it have on his or her spiritual life as a Christian?

_____

_____

_____

Imagine you are standing at the edge of a minefield that you *must* cross, and you hold in your hands two maps, each claiming to reveal the location of the mines. One is partially correct; the other is completely without error. And you don't know which is which. Describe your thoughts and emotions as you take your first step.

_____

_____

_____

_____

_____

DISCOVERING THE WAY

At least one purpose for John's Apocalypse was to provide a future, end-times generation with truth that would silence the lies of the devil. Nevertheless, the battle to win the minds of men and women continues to rage. According to a *Newsweek* poll conducted in 2004, only thirty-six percent of Americans believe that the book of Revelation contains "true prophecy." Forty-seven percent believe John's writings to be metaphorical.[1] But this skepticism is not new. Some early theologians struggled to accept the Apocalypse as Scripture, and even John himself seemed to understand that the vivid—even bizarre—images he saw and reported would be difficult for many to accept as a trustworthy revelation of truth. To confirm its credibility, John not only signed the document himself, but he called upon the testimony of two other witnesses: a heavenly messenger and the Son of God.

THE TESTIMONY OF AN ANGEL (REVELATION 22:6–7)

In Revelation 22:6, the pronoun *he* refers to the angel who guided John's vision of heaven (Revelation 21:9–10, 15–16; 22:1). Referring to both the incredible vision of the New Jerusalem and the content of Revelation as a whole, the angel verified the authenticity of John's words as "faithful and true." We can derive three exhortations from this passage.

First, *we are to believe what is faithful and true.*

Read Revelation 3:14 and 19:11. To what or to whom does the phrase "faithful and true" refer?

In Revelation 21:5 and 22:6, John uses the same phrase to describe "these words." How is this significant?

Information can never be more reliable than its source. For instance, the Internet allows people to distribute information faster and farther than ever before, which unfortunately gives genuine experts and charlatans the same advantage. So, anyone researching financial advice or medical information must always ask, *Is this a source I can trust?*

Because Jesus is "faithful and true," we must choose Him as our authoritative source of all knowledge. We are able to implicitly trust whatever He says.

Second, *we are to anticipate what has been predicted.*

Speaking through another prophet many centuries prior to John, the Lord encouraged His people with the words, "Truly I have spoken; truly I will bring it to pass. I have planned it, surely I will do it" (Isaiah 46:11). The angel's words tell us that not only will the events in Revelation surely come to pass, but they are imminent. The angel also relays the Lord's declaration, "Behold, I am coming quickly" (Revelation 22:7). We are to live in a constant state of readiness, not neglecting our duties or failing to prepare for the future, but always looking forward to the coming of Christ.

Third, *we are to heed what has been revealed.*

Prophecy is never given merely to satisfy humankind's desire to know the future. The primary purpose of prophecy is obedience; prophecy reveals how the faithful should behave when future events come to pass. And so the Apocalypse closes with the same assurance that introduced it: "Blessed is he who heeds the words of the prophecy of this book" (Revelation 22:7; see also 1:3).

THE TESTIMONY OF JOHN (REVELATION 22:8–11)

Much like the testimony of the angel, John's portion of the epilogue also can be divided into three separate parts:

First, *we are to respect the revealed Word of God.*

Who pronounces the blessing in Revelation 1:3? Who blesses those who heed in 22:7?

_____

_____

_____

What is the significance of Jesus repeating John's words?

_____

_____

_____

Read Revelation 22:8. What was John's reaction to the truth he saw revealed? Why do you think he reacted this way?

_____

_____

_____

In John's sense of wonder, we see a profound respect for the truth the Lord allowed him to see. Far greater than the opinion of any mere mortal, it is divinely inspired truth that is at the heart of the book of Revelation. This truth is at once too marvelous to comprehend and too important to ignore.

Second, *we are to reject the worship of anyone (or anything) other than the Lord our God.*

In Revelation 22:8, what or who is the object of John's worship?

_____

_____

_____

Why did the angel reprimand John in verse 9?

_____

_____

_____

The worship of God to the exclusion of all else is a consistent theme throughout the book of Revelation. John's first visions describe the worship of God by the heavenly host, and as the visions continue to unfold, worship punctuates key events. Then, in Revelation 13 and 14, the Beast threatens true worship by presenting himself as a god and demanding that the world treat him accordingly. Those who engage in the worship of anyone but God are subsequently condemned to suffer the same punishment as the Beast. Therefore, it is surprising that John would make the mistake of worshiping something other than God—not once, but twice (Revelation 19:10; 22:8–9).

John's impulsive worship of the wrong object merely illustrates the ease with which all people make the same error. How prone we are as humans to mistake the gift for the Giver when we receive a great blessing! Each time John worshiped something or someone other than the Lord, he received a stern rebuke that we would do well to remember: "Do not do that. . . . Worship God" (Revelation 22:9).

Third, _we are to remember the warnings._

John was told not to seal the book of prophecy because the time is near. The angel remarked to John, "Let the one who does wrong, still do wrong; and the one who is filthy, still be filthy; and let the one who is righteous, still practice righteousness; and the one who is holy, still keep himself holy" (Revelation 22:11). In other words, while the details are difficult to sort out, the choices have been made clear and the consequences explicit; let each person heed the warnings and choose wisely— while there is still time!

THE TESTIMONY OF JESUS (REVELATION 22:12–16)

Below the testimonies of the angel and John, Jesus undersigned the document, issuing four declarations, each of which summarizes a major message in the book of Revelation.

First, "Behold, I am coming quickly" (Revelation 22:7, 12).

After more than two thousand years, Jesus's declaration might appear to be a false statement. But the Greek term translated as "quickly" has less to do with rapid movement than the absence of delay. He will arrive in person as soon as any intervening events, known only to God, have taken place. For us, His coming is imminent. In essence, the Lord was saying, *My coming is sure, never late.*

Second, "My reward is with Me, to render to every man according to what he has done" (Revelation 22:12).

When the Lord Jesus comes again to Earth, He will bring justice to those who rejected His free offer of grace. The time for repentance will have ended. Each unsaved person will receive what he or she deserves for sin, without regard for fame, wealth, or status. In other words, Jesus was saying, *My rewards are just, never biased.*

Third, "I am the Alpha and the Omega, the first and the last, the beginning and the end" (Revelation 22:13).

In the Greek alphabet, *alpha* is the first letter and *omega* is the last. One commentator expressed the significance of Christ's self-designation this way: "An alphabet is an ingenious way to store and communicate knowledge. The 26 letters in the English alphabet, arranged in almost endless combinations, can hold and convey all knowledge. Christ is the supreme, sovereign alphabet."[2] He is the source of all that is true, so He can affirm with assurance, *My presence is transcendent, never irrelevant.*

Fourth, "Blessed are those who wash their robes, so that they may have the right to the tree of life, and may enter by the gates into the city. Outside are the dogs and the sorcerers and the immoral persons and the murderers and the idolaters, and everyone who loves and practices lying" (Revelation 22:14–15).

Jesus couples the final beatitude of the book of Revelation with a severe warning. Note the clear, "inside/outside" distinction—there's no ambiguous middle ground. Those who favor the relativism of postmodern philosophy reject such rigid categories as good versus bad and true versus false, especially as it relates to intangible matters like belief in Jesus. Of course the matter won't be so intangible upon Christ's physical return to Earth, which will validate what has been true all along: *My plan is clear, never vague.*

Jesus's last statement in this section of Scripture testifies to the truth of the book of Revelation, and with a grand flourish He endorses the document with His official signature:

> "I, Jesus, have sent My angel to testify to you these things for the churches. I am the root and the descendant of David, the bright morning star." (Revelation 22:16)

STARTING YOUR JOURNEY

When Jesus came to Earth two millennia ago, He came as light to a dark world (John 1:4–5), presenting clear, unambiguous truth. And we see in His words to first-century believers a timely reassurance for future generations: "If you continue in My word, then you are truly disciples of Mine; and you will know the truth, and the truth will make you free" (John 8:31–32).

Even though some may deny the very existence of truth, the power of truth is undeniable, as evidenced by these three observations:

First, *security comes from knowing the truth.*

Second, *faith is strengthened by believing the truth.*

Third, *courage is the result of acting on the truth.*

Earlier in the lesson you began a perilous journey across an imaginary minefield. Imagine now that one of the maps has been signed and notarized. You recognize the unmistakable signature of someone you trust, whose knowledge of the minefield is completely reliable. How does this affect your level of confusion? Or anxiety?

_____

_____

_____

As you gradually approach the opposite edge of the minefield, does your confidence in your chosen map increase or decrease?

_____

Having crossed several minefields successfully using the maps of your trustworthy friend, how do you regard minefields in general?

_____

_____

_____

How is this illustration analogous to the Bible and living as a Christian?

_____

_____

_____

❧

The relativist, postmodern model of truth would tell us that truth is subjective or an illusion, so we never have to worry about the negative consequences of choosing error. However, common sense declares this to be nonsense! No wonder so many people approach life with such trepidation, moving forward with tentative anxiety or standing still, frozen with fear that each step might cause suffering. The Christian can face the future with confidence and security because he or she has been given the truth in clear, unambiguous terms. We know the book of Revelation to be reliable because it bears the signed, sealed, sworn testimony of Jesus Christ.

LESSON FIFTEEN

COME, LORD JESUS

Revelation 22:17–21

THE HEART OF THE MATTER
Last words are often meaningful because they must be brief, and therefore they are chosen with great care. Such are the last few verses of the book of Revelation. Having written down the visions and certified their authenticity, the apostle John closed with a summary and clarification of the primary message of Revelation. His final words include an invitation, an exhortation, and a benediction. And each of these calls for a response.

In preparation for this lesson, read Revelation 22:17–21.

YOU ARE HERE
A person's last words often provide a glimpse into his or her character, sometimes revealing what he or she values most. Some parting comments are thoughtful; others are quite spontaneous and surprising. Here are the final utterances of a few well-known people in history:

"I shall hear in heaven. Clap now, my friends, the comedy is done."—Ludwig Van Beethoven, composer[1]

"I have been everything, and everything is nothing. A little urn will contain all that remains of one for whom the whole world was too little." —Severus, philosopher[2]

"Ah, is this dying? How I have dreaded as an enemy this smiling friend."—Thomas Goodwin, Puritan and president of Magdalen College, London[3]

"I've never felt better."—Douglas Fairbanks, actor[4]

"Don't let it end like this. Tell them I said something."—Pancho Villa, revolutionary[5]

"What an artist dies in me! It is now too late."—Nero, Roman emperor[6]

"Alas! I suppose I am turning into a god. An emperor should die standing" (and he stood).—Vespasian, Roman emperor[7]

"Read me something from the Bible, something brave and triumphant."—F. B. Meyer, preacher and author[8]

If you could script your final words on earth before going to meet the Lord, to whom would you say them and what message would you leave?

_____

_____

_____

_____

_____

If you could address the whole world with just a sentence or two, what would you say?

_____

_____

_____

_____

_____

If you remember the final words of someone significant to you, write them below.

_____

_____

_____

How have these words affected you?

_____

_____

 DISCOVERING THE WAY

Last words wield such influence because they do so much with so little. They have the ability to distill a lifetime—or a body of work—down to its essence, clarifying the ambiguous, solidifying the ethereal, prioritizing the random, and summarizing the minute. The last five verses of the book of Revelation represent the last God-breathed words we will receive until Christ returns. And in these few lines, the Spirit of Christ expresses the underlying purpose and message of the entire Apocalypse. This conclusion can be divided into three parts.

AN INVITATION (REVELATION 22:17)

First, Jesus speaks an *invitation* to all who are thirsty to "Come." (Revelation 22:17).

The entire book of Revelation is the message of Jesus Christ, delivered to John by the agency of an angel. And the Lord's ultimate reason for revealing future events is to draw all people to Himself. The implied invitation that is woven throughout the book is made explicit in the conclusion.

In Revelation 22:17, the "Spirit" obviously refers to the Holy Spirit, but what does the "bride" represent? (See Revelation 19:7–8; 21:2, 9.)

_____

_____

_____

DIGGING DEEPER
Come Quickly

"The Spirit and the bride say, 'Come'" (Revelation 22:17), but whom are they addressing? Are they calling out to unbelievers who need to come to Christ (like the call to the thirsty), or are they pleading for the Lord to come to earth?

John's specific choice of words and the subtleties of his Greek grammar suggest that the Holy Spirit and the church are joining their voices in a call for the Son's return. We understand why the church would cry, "Come," but why would the Spirit pray such a prayer when He, Himself, is God?

In Romans 8:19–22, Paul said that creation groans in painful anticipation of Christ's return, at which time He will put an end to the affliction of evil. In Romans 8:23–25, Paul affirmed that we, too, groan within ourselves, hoping to escape the pain of evil and enjoy the glory of His return. Furthermore, Paul encouraged us with the words, "In the same way the Spirit also helps our weakness; for we do not know how to pray as we should, but the Spirit Himself intercedes for us with groanings too deep for words; and He who searches the hearts knows what the mind of the Spirit is, because He intercedes for the saints according to the will of God" (Romans 8:26–27).

At least one ministry of the Holy Spirit involves petitioning the Father in the name of the Son, on behalf of believers. How marvelous is the provision of the Trinity! Even if we are too busy, too ignorant, or too hurt to pray, the Spirit of God within us will intercede on our behalf—which includes a desperate, agonized cry to the Son, "Come quickly, Lord Jesus!"

The final invitation in Revelation begins with the Holy Spirit prompting the church to anticipate the Son's return. What follows is an invitation to those throughout the ages who do not have a relationship with Jesus Christ, in which John says, in effect, *Join the Spirit and the bride in our call for His coming!* Note that this is not something the unbeliever can do without hastening his or her own destruction. Remember, the legions of the Beast's armies will someday gather at Armageddon in a vain attempt to prevent the Lord's return because He comes to destroy all those who reject His free offer of eternal life.

Note also that the invitation calls those who are thirsty, promising that Jesus will abundantly supply the living water that every person needs. John was reminding those who would read his words in the future that it is not yet too late. They may still respond to Jesus's gift.

The images of thirst and water are favorites of John's. Review these passages of Scripture in which he used these metaphors. Indicate how much the water costs in each example.

John 4:10–14 _____

John 7:37–39 _____

Revelation 7:14–17 _____

Revelation 21:6–7 _____

Revelation 22:1–4 _____

AN EXHORTATION (REVELATION 22:18–19)

The second part of John's conclusion is an *exhortation* (Revelation 22:18–19).

The "I" in "I testify" is emphatic in the Greek text and refers to Jesus, which adds the weight of divine authority to a very grave warning. These dual couplets—two if-then statements—give stern warning to anyone who would alter His Word.

Read Revelation 22:18–19 and complete each couplet in your own words.

If anyone adds _____

God will add _____

If anyone takes away _____

God will take away _____

This warning is similar to the words God spoke to the people of Israel as they began to settle the Promised Land: "You shall not add to the word which I am commanding you, nor take away from it, that you may keep the commandments of the Lord your God which I command you" (Deuteronomy 4:2).

It is conceivable that an ancient Israelite might be tempted to alter the physical written record of the Law, but unlikely. How else might someone "add to" or "take away from" the Bible? Can you think of more than one way someone might do this?

_____

_____

_____

_____

_____

Some well-meaning theologians argue that certain versions or paraphrases of the Bible violate the parameters given in Revelation 22:18–19. Still others argue that even errors made in good faith while attempting to interpret and apply Scripture constitute "adding to" or "taking away from" God's Word. While correct handling of Scripture is vital to the health of the church and while the Lord promises severe judgment for false teachers (James 3:1; Jude 11–13), the warning in Revelation 22:18 addresses neither issue. The principal concern in this exhortation—as it is throughout the book of Revelation—is *obedience*. One keeps the words of God by hearing, accepting, and internalizing them as he or she reflects the Lord's character by his or her deeds.

A BENEDICTION (REVELATION 22:20–21)

The final aspect of John's conclusion to the book of Revelation is a *benediction* (22:20–21).

The term *benediction* comes from the compound Latin word, *bene*, meaning "well," and *dicere*, meaning "to say." [9] The long-held custom of leaders has been to dismiss a congregation or close a letter with "a good word," a blessing. Here, at the very end of a very unsettling series of visions describing the fate of believers and unbelievers, none other than the Lord offers this word of reassurance: "Yes, I am coming quickly" (Revelation 22:20). Of all the last words Jesus could have chosen, He left us with these five (only three in Greek!). His coming is assured.

How many times does the Lord promise to come in Revelation 22? List the verses below.

_____

_____

_____

Read Revelation 22:20. What is John's immediate response to the Lord's last words? What emotions or thoughts might prompt such a response?

_____

_____

_____

The term *amen* is a Greek transliteration of a Hebrew exclamation (pronounced *ah-main*), which is based on the verb, "to confirm, support, uphold . . . to be certain." [10] A literal rendering could be, "May it be so!" John then added a phrase that is reminiscent of an Aramaic slogan that became popular among first-century Christians: "Maranatha," or "Our Lord, come!" (1 Corinthians 16:22).

Because the book of Revelation takes the form of a letter, it closes with a blessing typical of Christian correspondence in Scripture (Romans 16:24; Galatians 6:18). The late pastor and author J. Vernon McGee noted that the Old Testament concluded with a curse, while the New Testament ends with a blessing of grace. [11] And it is addressed to all, not just the church. Indeed, the grace of God is offered to everyone. Sadly, though the Lord invites the world to come, the majority will not heed His call.

STARTING YOUR JOURNEY

The book of Revelation was written during a very difficult time in Christian history. Domitian was the first Roman Emperor to officially deify himself, adopting the title "Lord and God." He did his best to see that everyone in the empire honored Rome's traditional religious practices. This involved persecuting such "atheists" as Jews and Christians, who worshiped a God who could not be seen. An easy way to identify these underground enemies was to demand that they worship the emperor as a condition of conducting business. As a result, many believers were martyred during this time.[12]

With the church under severe persecution and John banished to the desolate island of Patmos, the Lord gave suffering believers—of that time and the centuries to follow— a lengthy letter of hope and comfort. Revelation's vivid, striking images and dire predictions of doom for the world offer a strangely satisfying form of comfort. In effect, the persecuted righteous hear the Righteous Judge say, *Don't lose heart; remain faithful; I will vindicate your suffering soon.*

The concluding thoughts in this letter of comfort come in the form of an invitation, an exhortation, and a benediction, each of which summarizes a major theme for a particular audience. These can be expressed in three succinct statements.

To those who are lonely and lost: *Come!*

You are invited to receive God's abundant grace, the free offer of eternal life in heaven with Him.

To those who are indifferent or apathetic: *Wake up!*

Your present choices have eternal consequences, and Christ's return is imminent.

To those who are anxious and fearful: *Grace be with you!*

The Lord is sovereign, and He will preserve you to the end.

We must note once more that the book of Revelation offers comfort only to some, while predicting a terrifying outcome for others. In the words of the first beatitude in Revelation:

Blessed is he who reads and those who hear the words of the prophecy, and heed the things which are written in it; for the time is near.
(Revelation 1:3)

Are you ready? Describe in a few short sentences how you can be sure.

_____

_____

_____

_____

_____

_____

If you are unsure, read "How to Begin a Relationship with God" at the end of
this Bible Companion. We invite you to contact us if you have made or would like
to make a decision to accept Christ's offer of salvation by grace through faith in Him.
Call or write one of our seminary-trained pastors or counselors using the information
provided.

From all of us at Insight for Living: Grace be with you!

How to Begin a Relationship with God

Many people associate the book of Revelation with visions of fire and brimstone, but sometimes they forget that Revelation is filled with profound promises. To those who "overcome," Christ personally offers eternal life, a guaranteed inheritance, the prospects of reigning as royalty over the earth, and freedom from suffering, sorrow, and death (Revelation 2:7, 11, 17, 26; 3:5, 12, 21). Who are the ones who "overcome"? Are they super-saints who live unblemished lives? Do they work hard enough to earn their own reward? Have they suffered and died for the faith? Do they attend the right church and go through the right rituals? The apostle John makes it clear who these victorious ones really are: "Who is the one who overcomes the world, but he who believes that Jesus is the Son of God?" (1 John 5:5).

To understand how you can begin a relationship with God and join the number of those who "overcome," we need to back up from the end of the story and consider the beginning. The most marvelous book in the world, the Bible, marks the path to God with four vital truths. Let's look at each marker in detail.

Our Spiritual Condition: Totally Depraved

The first truth is rather personal. One look in the mirror of Scripture, and our human condition becomes painfully clear:

> There is none righteous, not even one;
> There is none who understands,
> There is none who seeks for God;
> All have turned aside, together they have become useless;
> There is none who does good,
> There is not even one. (Romans 3:10–12)

We are all sinners through and through—totally depraved. Now, that doesn't mean we've committed every atrocity known to humankind. We're not as *bad* as we can be, just as *bad off* as we can be. Sin colors all our thoughts, motives, words, and actions.

You still don't believe it? Look around. Everything around us bears the smudge marks of our sinful nature. Despite our best efforts to create a perfect world, crime statistics continue to soar, divorce rates keep climbing, and families keep crumbling.

Something has gone terribly wrong in our society and in ourselves—something deadly. Contrary to how the world would repackage it, "me-first" living doesn't equal rugged individuality and freedom; it equals death. As Paul said in his letter to the Romans, "The wages of sin is death" (Romans 6:23)—our spiritual and physical death that comes from God's righteous judgment of our sin, along with all of the emotional and practical effects of this separation that we experience on a daily basis. This brings us to the second marker: God's character.

GOD'S CHARACTER: INFINITELY HOLY

How can a good God judge the world with the wrath described in Revelation? To bring it closer to home, how can God judge each of us for a sinful state we were born into? Our total depravity is only half the answer. The other half is God's infinite holiness.

The fact that we know things are not as they should be points us to a standard of goodness beyond ourselves. Our sense of injustice in life on this side of eternity implies a perfect standard of justice beyond our reality. That standard and source is God Himself. And God's standard of holiness contrasts starkly with our sinful condition.

Scripture says that "God is Light, and in Him there is no darkness at all" (1 John 1:5). He is absolutely holy, which creates a problem for us. If He is so pure, how can we who are so impure relate to Him?

Perhaps we could try being better people, try to tilt the balance in favor of our good deeds, or seek out methods for self-improvement. Throughout history, people have attempted to live up to God's standard by keeping the Ten Commandments or living by their own code of ethics. Unfortunately, no one can come close to satisfying the demands of God's law. Romans 3:20 says, "For no one can ever be made right in God's sight by doing what his law commands. For the more we know God's law, the clearer it becomes that we aren't obeying it" (NLT).

OUR NEED: A SUBSTITUTE

So here we are, sinners by nature and sinners by choice, trying to pull ourselves up by our own bootstraps to attain a relationship with our holy Creator. But every time we try, we fall flat on our faces. We can't live a good enough life to make up for our sin, because God's standard isn't "good enough"—it's *perfection*. And we can't make amends for the offense our sin has created without dying for it.

Who can get us out of this mess?

If someone could live perfectly, honoring God's law, and would bear sin's death penalty for us—in our place—then we would be saved from our predicament. But is there such a person? Thankfully, yes!

Meet your substitute—*Jesus Christ*. He is the One who took death's place for you!

> [God] made [Jesus Christ] who knew no sin to be sin on our behalf, so that we might become the righteousness of God in Him. (2 Corinthians 5:21)

GOD'S PROVISION: A SAVIOR

God rescued us by sending His Son, Jesus, to die for our sins on the cross (1 John 4:9–10). Jesus was fully human and fully divine (John 1:1, 18), a truth that ensures His understanding of our weaknesses, His power to forgive, and His ability to bridge the gap between God and us (Romans 5:6–11). In short, we are "justified as a gift by His grace through the redemption which is in Christ Jesus" (Romans 3:24). Two words in this verse bear further explanation: *justified* and *redemption*.

Justification is God's act of mercy, in which He declares righteous the believing sinners while we are still in our sinning state. Justification doesn't mean that God *makes* us righteous so that we never sin again, rather that He *declares* us righteous— much like a judge pardons a guilty criminal. Because Jesus took our sin upon Himself and suffered our judgment on the cross, God forgives our debt and proclaims us PARDONED.

Redemption is Christ's act of paying the complete price to release us from sin's bondage. God sent His Son to bear His wrath for all of our sins—past, present, and future (Romans 3:24–26; 2 Corinthians 5:21). In humble obedience, Christ willingly endured the shame of the cross for our sake (Mark 10:45; Romans 5:6–8; Philippians 2:8). Christ's death satisfied God's righteous demands. He no longer holds our sins against us, because His own Son paid the penalty for them. We are freed from the slave market of sin, never to be enslaved again!

PLACING YOUR FAITH IN CHRIST

These four truths describe how God has provided a way to Himself through Jesus Christ. Because the price has been paid in full by God, we must respond to His free gift of eternal life in total faith and confidence in Him to save us. We must step forward into the relationship with God that He has prepared for us—not by doing good works or being a good person, but by coming to Him just as we are and accepting His justification and redemption by faith.

> For by grace you have been saved through faith; and that not of yourselves, it is the gift of God; not as a result of works, so that no one may boast. (Ephesians 2:8–9)

We accept God's gift of salvation simply by placing our faith in Christ alone for the forgiveness of our sins. Would you like to enter a relationship with your Creator by trusting in Christ as your Savior? If so, here's a simple prayer you can use to express your faith:

> *Dear God,*
>
> *I know that my sin has put a barrier between You and me. Thank You for sending Your Son, Jesus, to die in my place. I trust in Jesus alone to forgive my sins, and I accept His gift of eternal life. I ask Jesus to be my personal Savior and the Lord of my life. Thank You. In Jesus's name, amen.*

If you've prayed this prayer or one like it and you wish to find out more about knowing God and His plan for you in the Bible, contact us at Insight for Living. Our contact information is on the following pages.

As you ponder your personal destiny in light of the book of Revelation, no other decision can compare with the one that puts you in a right relationship with God through His Son, Jesus Christ, who loved us and gave Himself for us.

WE ARE HERE FOR YOU

If you desire to find out more about knowing God and His plan for you in the Bible, contact us. Insight for Living provides staff pastors who are available for free written correspondence or phone consultation. These seminary-trained and seasoned counselors have years of experience and are well-qualified guides for your spiritual journey.

Please feel welcome to contact your regional Pastoral Ministries by using the information below:

United States

Insight for Living
Pastoral Ministries
Post Office Box 269000
Plano, Texas 75026-9000
972-473-5097, Monday through Friday,
8:00 a.m. – 5:00 p.m. Central time
www.insight.org/contactapastor

Canada

Insight for Living Canada
Pastoral Ministries
Post Office Box 2510
Vancouver, BC V6B 3W7
CANADA
1-800-663-7639
info@insightforliving.ca

Australia, New Zealand, and South Pacific

Insight for Living Australia
Pastoral Care
Post Office Box 1011
Bayswater, VIC 3153
AUSTRALIA
1 300 467 444

United Kingdom and Europe

Insight for Living United Kingdom
Pastoral Care
Post Office Box 348
Leatherhead
KT22 2DS
UNITED KINGDOM
0800 915 9364
+44 (0) 1372 370 055
pastoralcare@insightforliving.org.uk

ENDNOTES

Unless otherwise noted below, all material in this Bible Companion is adapted from the *Revelation—Unveiling the End, Act 3: The Final Curtain* sermon series by Charles R. Swindoll and was supplemented by Creative Ministries of Insight for Living.

LESSON ONE

1. For various views on hell, see William Crockett, ed., *Four Views on Hell*, Counterpoints (Grand Rapids: Zondervan, 1996).

2. John F. Walvoord, "Revelation," in *The Bible Knowledge Commentary: New Testament Edition*, ed. John F. Walvoord and Roy B. Zuck (Wheaton, Ill.: Victor Books, 1988), 964. Copyright © 1988 by John Walvoord and Roy Zuck. Used by permission. To order: www.cookministries.com. All rights reserved.

LESSON TWO

1. James Swanson, *A Dictionary of Biblical Languages with Semantic Domains: Greek (New Testament)*, electronic ed. 2d ed. (Oak Harbor, Wash.: Logos Research Systems, 2001).

2. Robert L. Thomas, *Revelation 8–22: An Exegetical Commentary* (Chicago: Moody Press, 1995), 222.

3. W. E. Vine, Merrill F. Unger, and William White, *Vine's Complete Expository Dictionary of Old and New Testament Words* (Nashville: Thomas Nelson, 1996), 536.

4. John MacArthur, Jr., *Revelation 12–22,* The MacArthur New Testament Commentary (Chicago: Moody Press, 2000), 117–118.

5. Julia Ward Howe, "Battle Hymn of the Republic," in *The Hymnal for Worship and Celebration* (Waco, Tex.: Word Music, 1986), no. 569.

LESSON THREE

1. *The Strongest NASB Exhaustive Concordance* (Grand Rapids: Zondervan, 2000), 1558.

2. *The Strongest NASB Exhaustive Concordance*, 1558.

3. John Phillips, *Exploring Revelation*, rev. ed. (Chicago: Moody Press, 1987), 187.

4. Robert L. Thomas, *Revelation 8–22: An Exegetical Commentary* (Chicago: Moody Press, 1995), 243.

5. H. G. Liddell and Robert Scott, *An Intermediate Greek-English Lexicon: Founded upon the 7th ed. of Liddell and Scott's Greek-English Lexicon*, 1889 (Oxford: Clarendon Press, 1986), 861.

6. W. E. Vine, Merrill F. Unger, and William White, eds., *Vine's Complete Expository Dictionary of Old and New Testament Words* (Nashville: Thomas Nelson, 1985), 76.

7. A. W. Tozer, *The Divine Conquest* (Harrisburg, Penn.: Christian Publications, 1950), 23.

LESSON FOUR

1. Adapted from Barry J. Beitzel, *The Moody Atlas of Bible Lands* (Chicago: Moody Bible Institute of Chicago, 1985), 32. Copyright © 1985 by the Moody Bible Institute of Chicago. Used by permission.

2. James Henry Breasted, *Ancient Records of Egypt: Historical Documents* (Chicago: Russell & Russell, Inc., 1906), 185.

3. Paul J. Achtemeier, ed., *Harper's Bible Dictionary* (San Francisco: Harper & Row, 1985), 621.

4. Grant R. Osborne, *Revelation*, Baker Exegetical Commentary on the New Testament, ed. Moisés Silva (Grand Rapids: Baker Academic, 2002), 597.

LESSON FIVE

1. John F. Walvoord, "Revelation," in *The Bible Knowledge Commentary: New Testament Edition*, ed. John F. Walvoord and Roy B. Zuck (Wheaton, Ill.: Victor Books, 1988), 968. Copyright © 1988 by John Walvoord and Roy Zuck. Used by permission. To order: www.cookministries.com. All rights reserved.

2. John MacArthur, Jr., *Revelation 12–22*, The MacArthur New Testament Commentary (Chicago: Moody Press, 2000), 146–147.

3. M.G. Easton, *Easton's Bible Dictionary*, electronic ed. (Oak Harbor, Wash.: Logos Research Systems, 1996), see "Euphrates."

4. John F. Walvoord, "Revelation," in *The Bible Knowledge Commentary: New Testament Edition*, ed. John F. Walvoord and Roy B. Zuck (Wheaton, Ill.: Victor Books, 1988), 968. Copyright © 1988 by John Walvoord and Roy Zuck. Used by permission. To order: www.cookministries.com. All rights reserved.

Lesson Six

1. D. J. Wiseman, "Babylon," in *The International Standard Bible Encyclopedia*, vol. 1, *A–D*, ed. Geoffrey W. Bromiley and others (Grand Rapids: William B. Eerdmans, 1979), 385.

2. Allen P. Ross, "Genesis," in *The Bible Knowledge Commentary: Old Testament Edition*, ed. John F. Walvoord and Roy B. Zuck (Wheaton, Ill.: Victor Books, 1985), 44–45. Copyright © 1988 by John Walvoord and Roy Zuck. Used by permission. To order: www.cookministries.com. All rights reserved.

3. Allen P. Ross, "Genesis," in *The Bible Knowledge Commentary: Old Testament Edition*, ed. John F. Walvoord and Roy B. Zuck (Wheaton, Ill.: Victor Books, 1985), 44–45. Copyright © 1988 by John Walvoord and Roy Zuck. Used by permission. To order: www.cookministries.com. All rights reserved.

Lesson Seven

1. Alan Johnson, "Revelation," in *The Expositor's Bible Commentary*, vol. 12, *Hebrews–Revelation*, ed. Frank E. Gaebelein and J. D. Douglas (Grand Rapids: Zondervan, 1981), 568.

2. John Phillips, *Exploring Revelation*, rev. ed. (Chicago: Moody Press, 1987), 227.

3. John F. Walvoord, "Revelation," in *The Bible Knowledge Commentary: New Testament Edition*, ed. John F. Walvoord and Roy B. Zuck (Wheaton, Ill.: Victor Books, 1988), 975. Copyright © 1988 by John Walvoord and Roy Zuck. Used by permission. To order: www.cookministries.com. All rights reserved.

4. Renald E. Showers, *Maranatha Our Lord, Come! A Definitive Study of the Rapture of the Church* (Bellmawr, N.J.: The Friends of Israel Gospel Ministry, 1995), 164–169.

LESSON EIGHT

1. "Triumph," *Encyclopedia Britannica*, electronic ed., www.britannica.com/eb/article -9073447, accessed Sept. 6, 2006.

2. Robert Payne, *The Roman Triumph* (London: Abelard-Schuman, 1962), 41.

3. Anthony Miller, *Roman Triumphs and Early Modern English Culture* (Houndmills, Basingstoke, Hampshire, New York: Palgrave, 2001), 1.

4. Miller, *Roman Triumphs*, 19.

5. Payne, *The Roman Triumph*, 13.

6. Miller, *Roman Triumphs*, 37.

7. Payne, *The Roman Triumph*, 14.

8. Grant R. Osborne, *Revelation*, Baker Exegetical Commentary on the New Testament, ed. Moisés Silva (Grand Rapids: Baker Academic, 2002), 687.

9. John MacArthur, *The MacArthur Study Bible* (Nashville: Thomas Nelson, 1997), 2020.

LESSON NINE

1. Robert A. Pyne, *Humanity and Sin: The Creation, Fall, and Redemption of Humanity*, Swindoll Leadership Library, ed. Charles R. Swindoll (Nashville: Word Publishing, 1999), 223.

2. For various views on the Millennium, see Robert G. Clouse, ed., *The Meaning of the Millennium: Four Views* (Downers Grove, Ill.: InterVarsity, 1977).

3. For a defense of the literal view of the Millennium, see John F. Walvoord, *End Times: Understanding Today's World Events in Biblical Prophecy*, Swindoll Leadership Library, ed. Charles R. Swindoll (Nashville: Word Publishing, 1998), 185–205.

Lesson Ten

1. John MacArthur, *Revelation 12–22*, MacArthur New Testament Commentary (Chicago: Moody Press, 2000), 245.

2. Donald Grey Barnhouse, *Revelation: An Expositional Commentary* (Grand Rapids: Zondervan, 1971), 391.

3. MacArthur, *Revelation 12–22*, 245–246.

Lesson Eleven

1. "The Shorter Catechism," *The Westminster Standards* (Philadelphia: Great Commission Publications), 71.

2. "The Shorter Catechism," *The Westminster Standards*, 71.

3. Gerhard Kittel, ed., *Theological Dictionary of the New Testament*, Vol. 3, ed. and trans. Geoffrey W. Bromiley (Grand Rapids: William B. Eerdmans, 1967), 447.

4. David J. MacLeod, *The Seven Last Things: An Exposition of Revelation 19–21* (Dubuque, Iowa: Emmaus College Press, 2003), 248–249.

5. Robert L. Thomas, *Revelation 8–22: An Exegetical Commentary* (Chicago: Moody Press, 1995), 433.

6. *The International Standard Bible Encyclopedia*, Vol. 4 (Grand Rapids: William B. Eerdmans, 1988), 366.

7. Thomas, *Revelation 8–22: An Exegetical Commentary*, 440.

8. G. K. Beale, *The Book of Revelation: A Commentary on the Greek Text* (Grand Rapids: William B. Eerdmans, 1999), 1042.

9. *Merriam-Webster's Collegiate Dictionary*, 10th ed. (Springfield, Mass.: Merriam-Webster, 2000), see "glorify."

LESSON TWELVE

1. Grant R. Osborne, *Revelation*, Baker Exegetical Commentary on the New Testament, ed. Moisés Silva (Grand Rapids: Baker Academic, 2002), 749.

2. John MacArthur, Jr., *Revelation 12–22*, The MacArthur New Testament Commentary (Chicago: Moody Press, 2000), 279.

3. John Phillips, *Exploring Revelation*, rev. ed. (Chicago: Moody Press, 1987), 254.

LESSON THIRTEEN

1. Jim Elliot, quoted in Elisabeth Elliot, *Through Gates of Splendor*, Living Books ed. (Wheaton, Ill.: Tyndale House, 1981), 256.

2. Jim Elliot, *The Journals of Jim Elliot*, ed. Elisabeth Elliot (Grand Rapids: Fleming H. Revell, 2003), 309.

LESSON FOURTEEN

1. David Gates, "The Pop Prophets," *Newsweek*, May 24, 2004, 48.

2. John MacArthur, Jr., *The MacArthur Bible Commentary* (Nashville: Thomas Nelson, 2005), 1993.

LESSON FIFTEEN

1. Ludwig Van Beethoven, quoted in *Last Words of Saints and Sinners*, ed. Herbert Lockyer (Grand Rapids: Kregel, 1975), 117.

2. Severus, quoted in *Last Words of Saints and Sinners*, 76.

3. Thomas Goodwin, quoted in *Last Words of Saints and Sinners*, 56.

4. Douglas Fairbanks, quoted in *Famous Last Words: Fond Farewells, Deathbed Diatribes, and Exclamations upon Expiration*, ed. Roy Robinson (New York: Workman, 2003), 1.

5. Pancho Villa, quoted in *Famous Last Words*, 177.

6. Nero, quoted in *Last Words of Saints and Sinners*, 75.

7. Vespasian, quoted in *Last Words of Saints and Sinners*, 76.

8. F. B. Meyer, quoted in *Last Words of Saints and Sinners*, 72–73.

9. *Merriam-Webster's Collegiate Dictionary*, 10th ed. (Springfield, Mass.: Merriam-Webster, 2000), see "benediction."

10. R. Laird Harris, Gleason L. Archer, Jr., and Bruce K. Waltke, eds., *Theological Wordbook of the Old Testament*, vol. 1 (Moody Press: Chicago, 1980), 51.

11. J. Vernon McGee, *Thru the Bible with J. Vernon McGee*, vol. 5, *1 Corinthians – Revelation* (Nashville: Thomas Nelson, 1981), 1080. [Reference Only]

12. A. M. Renwick, "Roman Law," in *The International Standard Bible Encyclopedia*, vol. 4, *Q–Z*, rev. ed., ed. Geoffrey W. Bromiley and others (Grand Rapids: William B. Eerdmans, 1988), 217.

RESOURCES FOR PROBING FURTHER

For those who want to probe further into God's plan for the future, we recommend the following books written or edited by Bible-believing scholars.

GENERAL WORKS ON THE END TIMES

Benware, Paul N. *Understanding End Times Prophecy: A Comprehensive Approach*. Chicago: Moody, 1995.

Peterson, Eugene H. *Reversed Thunder: The Revelation of John and the Praying Imagination*. San Francisco: HarperSanFrancisco, 1988.

Swindoll, Charles R., J. Dwight Pentecost, and John F. Walvoord. *The Road to Armageddon: A Biblical Understanding of Prophecy and End Time Events*. Nashville: Word, 1999.

Walvoord, John F. *End Times: Understanding Today's World Events in Biblical Prophecy*. Swindoll Leadership Library, ed. Charles R. Swindoll. Dallas: Word, 1998.

Zuck, Roy B., ed. *Vital Prophetic Issues: Examining Promises and Problems in Eschatology*. Grand Rapids: Kregel, 1995.

COMMENTARIES AND REFERENCE WORKS ON THE BOOK OF REVELATION

Couch, Mal, ed. *A Bible Handbook to Revelation*. Grand Rapids: Kregel, 2001.

Ryrie, Charles C. *Revelation*. New ed. Everyman's Bible Commentary. Chicago: Moody, 1996.

Stedman, Ray C., and James D. Denney. *God's Final Word: Understanding Revelation*. Grand Rapids: Discovery House, 1991.

Thomas, Robert L. *Revelation 8–22: An Exegetical Commentary*. Ed. Kenneth Barker and Moisés Silva. Chicago: Moody, 1995.

Walvoord, John F. *The Revelation of Jesus Christ*. Chicago: Moody, 1966.

Differing Views on Revelation and the End Times

Archer, Gleason L., Jr., ed. *Three Views on the Rapture: Pre-, Mid-, or Post-Tribulation.* Grand Rapids: Zondervan, 1996.

Bock, Darrell L., ed. *Three Views on the Millennium and Beyond.* Grand Rapids: Zondervan, 1999.

Erickson, Millard J. *A Basic Guide to Eschatology: Making Sense of the Millennium.* Rev. ed. Grand Rapids: Baker Book House, 1998.

Pate, C. Marvin., ed. *Four Views on the Book of Revelation.* Grand Rapids: Zondervan, 1998.

Ordering Information

Revelation—Unveiling the End, Act 3
The Final Curtain

If you would like to order additional Bible Companions or purchase the audio series that accompanies this Bible Companion, please contact the office that serves you.

United States
Insight for Living
Post Office Box 269000
Plano, Texas 75026-9000
USA
1-800-772-8888
(Monday through
Friday 7:00 a.m. – 7:00 p.m.
Central time)
www.insight.org
www.insightworld.org

Canada
Insight for Living Canada
Post Office Box 2510
Vancouver, BC V6B 3W7
CANADA
1-800-663-7639
www.insightforliving.ca

Australia, New Zealand, and South Pacific
Insight for Living Australia
Post Office Box 1011
Bayswater, VIC 3153
AUSTRALIA
1300 467 444
www.insight.asn.au

United Kingdom and Europe
Insight for Living United Kingdom
Post Office Box 348
Leatherhead
KT22 2DS
UNITED KINGDOM
0800 915 9364
www.insightforliving.org.uk

Other International Locations
International constituents may contact the U.S. office through our Web site (www.insightworld.org), mail queries, or by calling +1-972-473-5136.